Nils Johnson III
RD#3, Box 11
Kutztown, PA., 19530
(1978)

A Gift From:
Karen & Steve Griffin

Advanced Furniture Construction

By the Same Author:
Amateur Furniture Construction
The Repair and Reupholstering of Old Furniture
The World of Sound
Amateur Cabinetmaking

Advanced Furniture Construction

by

Vernon M. Albers

South Brunswick and New York: A. S. Barnes and Company
London: Thomas Yoseloff Ltd

A. S. Barnes and Co., Inc.
Cranbury, New Jersey 08512

Thomas Yoseloff Ltd
108 New Bond Street
London W1Y OQX, England

Library of Congress Cataloging in Publication Data

Albers, Vernon Martin, 1902-
Advanced furniture construction.

1. Furniture making—Amateurs' manuals. I. Title.
TT195.A42 684.1 78-37822
ISBN 0-498-01110-0

Printed in the United States of America

Contents

Introduction

In my book, *Amateur Furniture Construction,* I described the basic joints and procedures for constructing simple furniture. In general, the kinds of furniture described can be constructed without the use of power tools, except where a turning lathe is required, although power tools can be used to advantage to reduce the amount of labor involved.

There are furniture construction problems which the amateur will not be able to handle without the use of power tools. It is true that these problems were handled by the early craftsmen with hand tools, but these craftsmen had hand tools available which are not readily available to the modern amateur, and it is doubtful if many amateurs could develop the necessary skills to do these operations entirely by hand. The early craftsmen learned their skills by serving a long apprenticeship.

It is not too difficult for an amateur to construct a fairly large chest of drawers with relatively simple equipment, but an examination of an ordinary chair will indicate that there are a number of problems which make construction of any but the most primitive chairs quite complicated.

It is sometimes possible to purchase pre-cut moldings for furniture that uses moldings. For example, there are kits available for building grandfather clocks which have all of the moldings preformed so that it is necessary only to cut the necessary miters to make the moldings to go around the three sides of the clock frame. It is, however, much more fun to cut the moldings yourself and you then have the freedom to use any kind of lumber to construct the clock. The early craftsmen had special planes with various interchangeable blades for forming moldings; but, a high degree of skill is required for their use and such planes are not readily available. It is much easier to cut such moldings with molding-cutter attachments on a saw, router or drill press.

Turned legs for tables are relatively easy to form on a simple wood turning lathe. Fluted legs and roped legs are much more difficult to form and special techniques are required to fabricate them.

In this book, I will describe the techniques and tools for constructing the various kinds of chairs, the methods of cutting straight and curved moldings, bending lumber, forming special table legs that are not simple turnings, and making accurately mitered frames. I will also describe the techniques necessary for fabricating special doors that involve a combination of curved and straight elements such as are often required for the face doors of clocks.

Advanced Furniture Construction

1

Chairs

1.1. Introduction

There are many kinds and shapes of chairs. Primitive chairs were made with the spacing between the back legs the same as that between the front legs and the legs were all vertical. Most chairs, however, are made with the spacing between the back legs less than that between the front legs.

The front legs are usually, but not always, vertical. The back legs usually extend upwards above the seat to form the back of the chair. In order to provide stability, the back legs usually extend to the rear of the seat at the bottom and, to provide comfort for the sitter, the top of the back also usually extends to the rear of the seat. If a single piece of wood forms the back leg and the back it will be necessary to form the piece approximately as indicated in Fig. 1.1. If this piece is cut from a piece of lumber the necessary shape can be cut with a band saw. If the piece is turned, it will be necessary to bend it after it is turned.

Because of the shapes of chairs, nearly all of the joints must be made at odd angles. This is one factor that makes chair construction so difficult. A chair is a relatively light structure and it is called on to support heavy loads so that

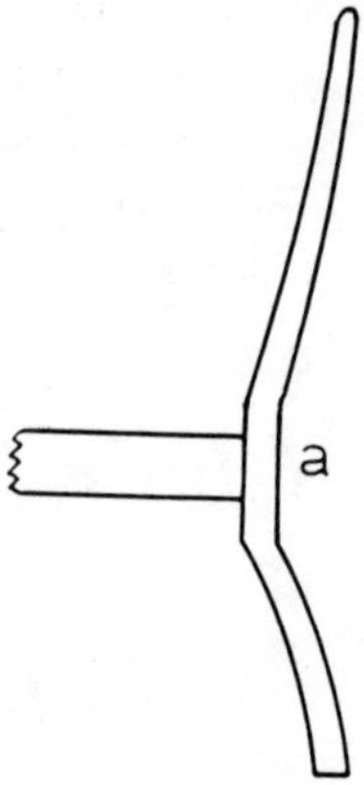

Fig. 1.1. Typical shape of a back leg of a chair where the back and the back leg are cut from a single piece of lumber.

all joints must be accurately constructed in order to provide the necessary strength.

1.2. Mortise and Tenon Joints

Figure 1.2 shows two common arrangements for forming

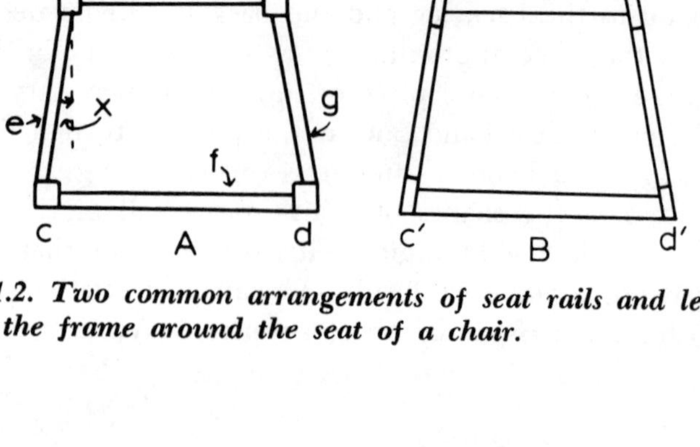

Fig. 1.2. Two common arrangements of seat rails and legs to form the frame around the seat of a chair.

the frame around the seat of a chair. In Fig. 1.2A, the rails joining the two back legs and the two front legs are perpendicular to the surfaces of the legs. If mortise and tenon joints are used at the ends of these rails, the mortises will be cut perpendicular to the surfaces of the legs and the method of making the joint is that described in *Amateur Furniture Construction.*

The joints at the ends of the rails joining the front legs to the back legs, where the rails make the angle *x* with the perpendicular to the front and back rails, will require mortises cut at the angle *x*. Figure 1.3 shows the detail of the joints at the leg *c* in Fig. 1.2A.

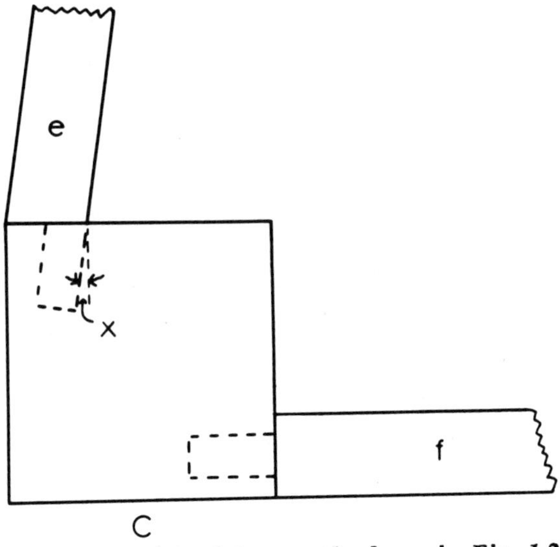

Fig. 1.3. Detail of the joints at the leg* c *in Fig. 1.2 A.

To form the tenon on the side rail *e,* it is necessary to accurately cut the surface which contacts the surface of the leg *c* at the angle *x*. This can best be done on a power saw by tilting the arbor to the angle *x* and making the cut with the saw height set just to the tenon as indicated in Fig. 1.4. Here *S* is the saw, *T* is the saw table and *e* is the rail. The wood beyond the saw cut will eventually be removed with a chisel. Note that the tenon is formed at the back of the rail instead of at the center. This is necessary because a tenon formed at the center of the rail would extend too near to the outside of the leg because of the angle at which the mortise will have to be cut.

The angle *x* can be calculated by use of trigonometry from the dimensions of the chair at the seat. It can also be determined by drawing the cross section shown in Fig. 1.2, accurately, full size on a large sheet of paper and using a protractor to measure the angle *x*. The angle scale on a power saw is often relatively coarse so you should cut a piece of scrap lumber and check the angle of cut to be certain that the saw cuts at the proper angle before making the cut indicated in Fig. 1.4. When the saw is finally set to

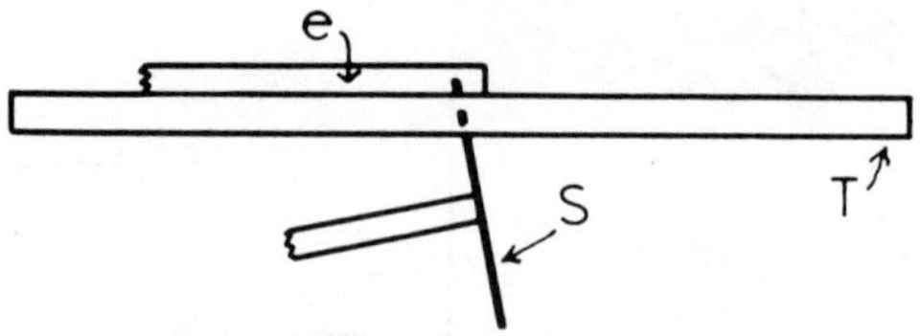

Fig. 1.4. Arrangement of the saw for making the cut to form the tenon on a seat rail.

the proper angle, the necessary cuts should be made for the four tenons on the two rails *e* and *g*. The tenon for the end of rail *e* which fits the mortise on the front leg is cut at the orientation shown in Fig. 1.4. The tenon for the other end of this rail will be cut with the rail at the other side of the saw and this will also be the orientation for cutting the tenon for the front end of rail *g*. The back end of rail *g* will be cut with the orientation shown in Fig. 1.4.

Before disturbing the angle setting of the saw arbor, you should raise the saw so that you can cut a strip from a piece of scrap lumber, as indicated in Fig. 1.5, which you will use when you make the mortises which will be cut at an angle in the legs.

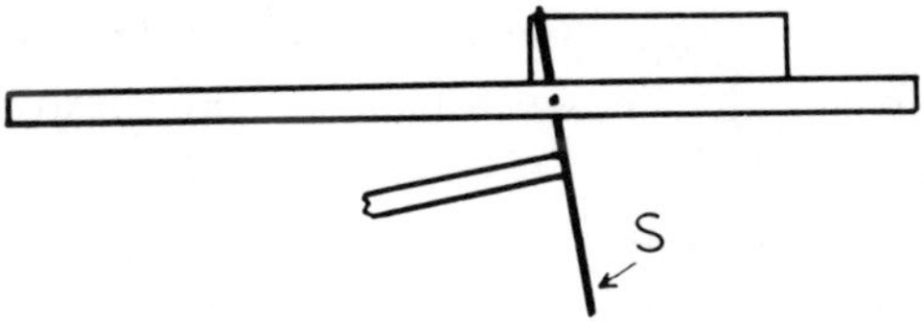

Fig. 1.5. Method of cutting a jig block for use in cutting a mortise at an angle other than 90 degrees.

When the cuts have been made for forming the tenons and, before removing the wood from the sides of the tenons, you should carefully lay out the location of the mortises. If the side rails of the chair are 3/4 inch thick and the tenon is to be 3/8 inch thick, the outside edge of the tenon will be slightly more than 3/8 inch because of the angle *x*. You can determine this dimension from your full scale layout. When the positions of the mortises are drawn on the legs, the arrangement shown in Fig. 1.6 is used on the drill press for drilling the mortises. The mortising tool is shown at M. (If you do not have a mortising attachment for your drill press, M would be a drill for drilling a series of holes so that the mortise can be made with a chisel.) The leg is shown at *c* and *a* is the jig block shown in Fig. 1.5. The drill press table is indicated at *T* and *b* is a temporary fence clamped to the drill press table to keep the leg *c* and

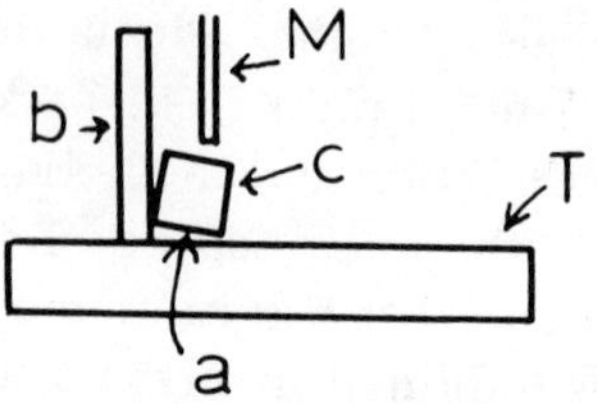

Fig. 1.6. Method of using a jig block in cutting an angle mortise in a chair leg.

the block *a* in the proper orientation. The stop on the drill press spindle should be set for the depth desired for the mortise.

In some instances, it is desirable to have the height of the tenon less than the total width of the rail as indicated in Fig. 1.7 A. The portion of the cut at *a* in Fig. 1.7 B can be cut on the power saw with the arbor set at the angle *x*.

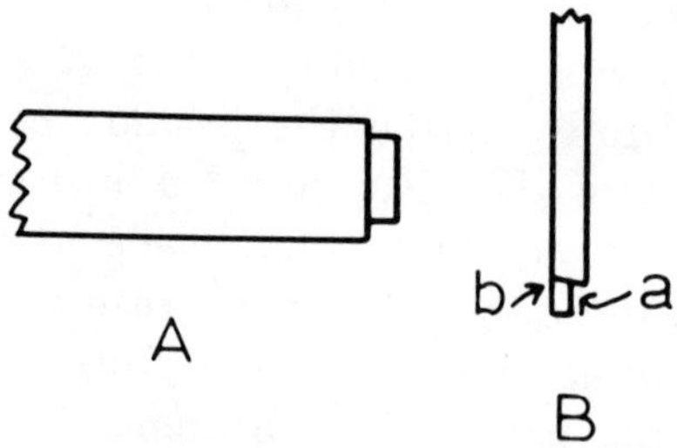

Fig. 1.7. Method of cutting off a top or bottom portion of a tenon which will be used in a mortise cut at an angle.

The wood from the region *b* in Fig. 1.7 A can be removed by making the cut *b* indicated in Fig. 1.7 B with a small hand back saw, using the surface *a* as a guide to keep the angle correct.

If the structure of the chair is like that shown in Fig. 1.2 B, all of the procedures are similar to those described for the arrangement in Fig. 1.2 A except that the joints on the front and back rails will be made at an angle and those on the side rails will be straight.

1.3. Stretchers

The stretchers are the elements which join the legs below the seat. Some more delicate chairs do not have stretchers. Most chairs have stretchers joining the front to the back legs and stretchers joining the front legs and also joining the back legs. In some instances there is a stretcher joining the centers of those which join the front to the back legs.

If the stretchers are rectangular pieces, they will be mortised into the legs in the same manner as the seat rails. Often these stretchers are turned spindles, sometimes straight turnings and sometimes ornamental. The ends of the spindles should be turned to a smaller diameter to fit holes which will be bored in the legs. The holes will need to be bored at an angle and this angle can best be determined from a full scale layout. In some instances the angle will be the same as that of the mortises for the seat rails.

1.4. Backs

In Fig. 1.1, the portion of the back leg at *a* is vertical and the portion above *a* may be straight with a backward slant or it may be curved as indicated in Fig. 1.1. The back legs are usually closer together at the bottom than at the top but, in some instances, the spacing is the same at the bottom as at the top. Usually the front to back width of the leg will decrease toward the top from the point *a* in Fig. 1.1.

Some chairs have legs which are thicker from side to side

at the bottom than at the top. The outside of the leg is ordinarily straight and the variation in width is made on the inside surface of the leg.

The back may consist of a top rail joining the tops of the legs with a thin vertical splat, often ornamental, between the seat rail and the top rail. The vertical splat may be straight from top to bottom or it may follow a curve similar to the curvature of the back legs. Chairs with low backs usually have a straight splat while chairs with high backs are more apt to have a curved splat. If the splat is curved, it should be bent, although it could be cut to the curved shape on a large band saw. However, few amateurs would have a band saw large enough to saw out a curved splat. Methods of bending lumber will be described in Chapter 3.

Chairs which do not have a vertical splat will have two or more curved rails between the legs above the back seat rail. These rails will usually be curved on the top and bottom edges and they will also be curved on the front and back sides. The ends of the rails will be mortised into the sides of the legs.

The fabrication of the back rails must be done in the proper sequence to insure a proper fit of the tenons into the mortises cut in the legs.

Figure 1.8 shows the piece of lumber from which a back

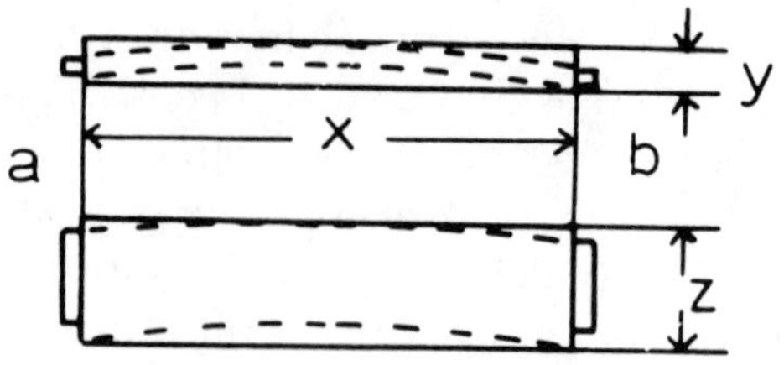

Fig. 1.8. Method of forming a curved back rail for a chair.

rail will be cut. The dimension *x* is equal to the distance between the back legs at the point where the rail will be located. The total length of the piece of lumber will be equal to *x* plus the lengths of the two tenons. The thickness *y* is determined by the amount of curvature of the rail and its thickness. The rails are usually about 1/2 inch thick and, for most chairs, the thickness *y* will need to be about 1 1/8 inch. The width *z* will be determined by the curvature in the vertical plane and the width of the rail. Typical widths are 3 to 4 inches.

The first step is to perform the cuts on the ends *a* and *b* to form the tenons. In some instances, these cuts will be perpendicular to the axis of the piece but in others there will be a slight angle in one or both planes which can be determined in the same manner as the angles on the ends of the seat rails *e* and *g* in Fig. 1.2 are determined. The mortise and tenon joints are usually made 1/4 inch wide and, if the inside surfaces of the legs are parallel, the mortises are not made at an angle. However, if the inside surfaces of the legs are not parallel as in Fig. 1.2 B, the angle at which the mortises are cut will be the same as the angles at which the mortises of the back seat rail were cut. The same jig block can therefore be used for cutting these mortises at the correct angle.

After the mortises are cut and the tenons are fitted to them, the piece of lumber should be placed on edge and cut along the dotted lines in the upper part of Fig. 1.8 with a band saw. Since the radius of curvature of these cuts is quite large a 1/4 inch or a 3/8 inch band saw blade can be used. The upper guide on the band saw blade should be adjusted close above the piece. The lines to be followed in the cut are usually arcs of circles, the radius of which will be specified in the particular design being copied.

The top and bottom curves shown in the lower half of

Fig. 1.8 should be cut on the band saw after the cuts shown in the upper half of the figure have been made.

When the four band saw cuts have been made, the rail should be finally shaped with files, scrapers and sandpaper. The top edge of the rail is usually rounded, while the bottom edge is left square as indicated in Fig. 1.9 which is a cross section of a typical rail when it is finished.

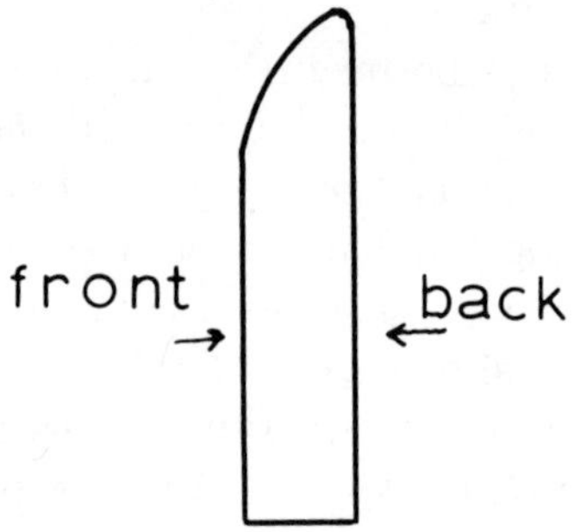

Fig. 1.9. Final shaping of a back rail for a chair.

The top rail on a chair which has a splat back serves the purpose of supporting the top end of the splat and the top ends of the legs. Figure 1.10 shows the top rail of a Queen Anne chair described by Ernest Carlyle Lynch, Jr. in his book, *Furniture Antiques Found in Virginia,* published by Bruce Publishing Co., Milwaukee (1954). The line from *a* to *a'* is a straight line forming the bottom edge of the piece from which this rail is cut. A tenon is cut on the top ends of each of the legs and mortises are cut in the bottom of the rail to match the tenons on the legs. A mortise is also cut in the center portion of the rail to receive the top end of the splat. The legs are closer together at the bottom than at the top so that the outside edges of the legs make an

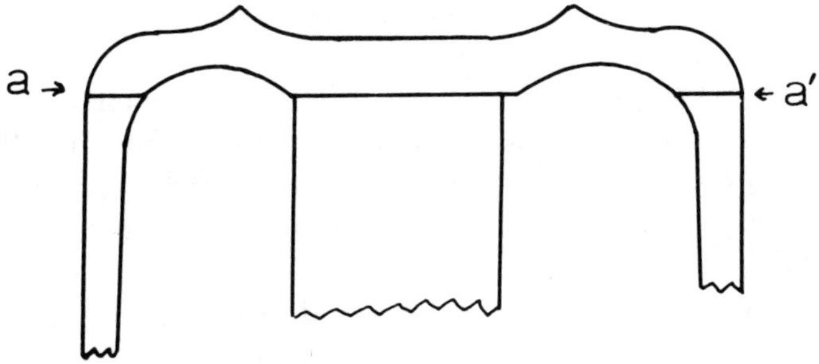

Fig. 1.10. Method of forming the top rail of a chair which has a vertical back splat.

angle of about 1 1/2 degrees with the vertical. In forming the tenons on the tops of the legs the cut must be made as shown in Fig. 1.11 where the angle *a* is 88 1/2 degrees. It is necessary to make the cuts for the tenons with a small back saw. Figure 1.11 B shows the angle of the cut *b* perpendicular to the cut *a*. In most instances the angle *b* will be 90 degrees.

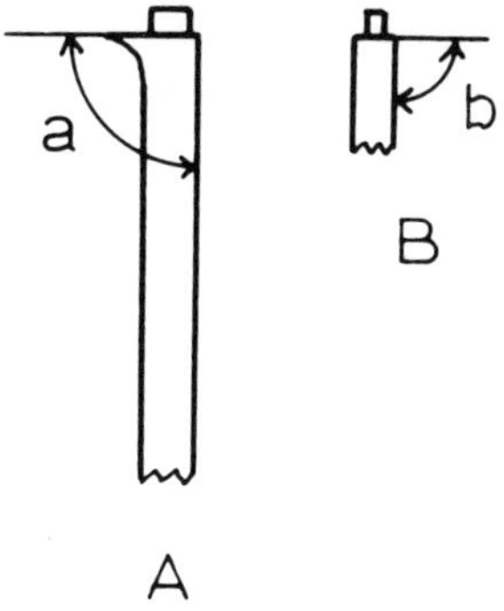

Fig. 1.11. Method of cutting a tenon on the top of a leg for the back rail.

1.5. Windsor Type Chairs

There are many designs of Windsor type chairs. They are similar in that they have a solid wood seat, usually of the order of 1 1/2 inches thick which has a depression scooped out in the central area to make the seat more comfortable. The legs and the spindles which support a top back rail are turned. In some Windsor chairs, the top back rail consists of a single bent piece extending from the seat on one side, around over the back and down to the seat on the other side.

The legs and the top spindles are all mounted in the seat at angles which are different in the front to back direction than in the side to side direction. The angles of the back legs may or may not be the same as the angles of the front legs. The holes in the seat which receive the ends of the legs and the spindles must be bored and the ends of the legs and spindles can be turned so that they fit snugly into the holes.

In order to drill the holes at the correct angles, one of the angles can be set with the tilting adjustment on the drill press table and the other can be set by means of a tapered jig block which you can cut on the table saw with the saw arbor set at the correct angle as shown in Fig. 1.5. The outline of the seat should, of course, be cut out before drilling the holes but the outside edges should not be shaped and the center area should not be scooped out until after the holes are bored.

Suppose the side to side angle of a front leg is 103 degrees and the front to back angle is 100 degrees. You can cut a 10 degree jig block ($100° - 90°$) and tilt the drill press table 13 degrees ($103° - 90°$) and place the seat on the drill press table, bottom side up, with the front to back axis of the seat parallel to the front to back axis of the drill press table. Most drill press tables have an angle scale which can be used for setting the angle of the table. If possible, the hole should be bored with a wood cutting bit. Usually the holes for the legs are bored completely through the seat because, in most instances, the ends of the legs project through to the top surface of the seat. However, there are some instances where the legs do not project through to the top surface of the seat. In such instances, the stop on the drill press spindle must be carefully set to insure that the holes are bored to the correct depth.

The back spindle holes are not usually bored all the way through the seat and the angles at which they are bored are not the same for all of the spindles. If there are an odd number of spindles, the side to side angle of the center spindle will be 90 degrees and corresponding spindles on each side of center will be at the same angles. This means that for a chair with seven spindles, four different jig blocks will have to be cut and there will be three different angles of tilt of the drill press table on each side of the normal 90 degree setting.

The two outside spindles are usually larger than the others, so the two outside holes will need to be larger than the other spindle holes.

It will be necessary to bore the holes in the legs for the stretchers at various odd angles. In order to hold the legs so that the holes can be bored in the center, they should be held in a standard Vee block on the drill press table and the correct angle can be set by tilting the drill press table. When the holes for the stretchers are bored and the stretchers are turned, the ends of the stretchers are turned to snugly fit the holes.

The bottom portion of the chair, including the seat, legs and stretchers should be glued together before the edges of the seat are shaped and the center portion is scooped out.

The legs should have saw kerfs cut in their top ends perpendicular to the grain of the seat. These kerfs should be cut to a depth about equal to the thickness of the seat and thin wedges should be made which can be coated with glue and driven into the kerfs when the legs are glued into the bottom of the seat.

The old craftsmen made the chair seat from a piece of lumber which was relatively green while the other parts were made from well dried lumber. After the chair is completely glued together the seat will gradually dry out and shrink so that it will grip the tops of the legs and the bottom ends of the back spindles more firmly as time goes on. If some fairly green lumber can be obtained for making the seat, this property can be utilized to make a stronger structure.

After the parts below the seat have been glued together, the seat should be scooped out to shape it and the edges should be shaped before the back is glued in place. The methods of scooping out the seat and forming the edges will be described in the next chapter.

1.6. Chairs with Arms

There are many kinds of chairs that have arms. It is not possible to describe all kinds of chairs with arms here but the techniques for the special angle cuts necessary would be similar to the techniques already described for fabricating other parts of chairs.

2

Special Shaping Problems

2.1. Introduction

There are many instances where considerable wood must be removed from a furniture part where it is not possible to use a saw or a plane. The tools to be used for such operations include gouges, rasps, files and scrapers. Occasionally a draw knife may be used.

If the wood is to be removed to form a depression in the surface, it is not possible to use a rasp, file or draw knife, so gouges and scrapers must be used. If, however, the surface to be formed is convex, rasps and files are usually the most effective means of shaping the surface.

2.2. The Draw Knife

It is seldom necessary to use a draw knife. However, it is an effective tool to remove wood to form a convex surface. Great care must be exercised in its use to avoid doing more harm than good. Figure 2.1 shows the orientation of a draw knife blade in use. If the grain of the wood runs as indicated in Fig. 2.1, the draw knife blade, indicated at *A*, should be drawn in the direction of the arrow. If the blade

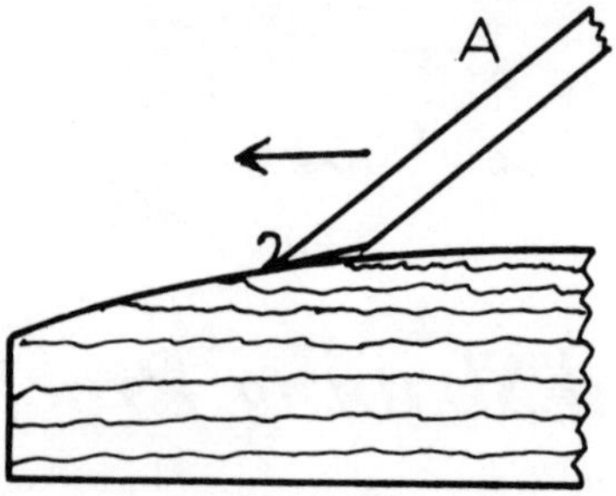

Fig. 2.1. Use of a draw knife in shaping wood. The blade of the knife is indicated at A and the arrow shows the direction of draw. The wavy lines indicate the direction of the wood grain.

is drawn in the opposite direction, it will bite into the grain and cause the wood to split or chip.

The blade of the draw knife must be kept very sharp and it should be controlled to cut a thin shaving on each draw. Considerable practice is required to produce a smooth cut with a draw knife, as the entire control of the depth of cut must be done with the handles. It is, of course, important to anchor the piece of lumber securely in a vise. I have found that irregular shaped pieces which cannot be readily clamped in a vise can often be held between centers in a lathe. When this is done, it is necessary to lock the headstock shaft so that the piece cannot turn while it is being worked on.

2.3. Rasps

Probably the most important tools for shaping convex surfaces are rasps. Most of the wood rasps are shaped, in cross section, as indicated in Fig. 2.2. If the surface to be formed is convex in one plane and concave in the other,

Fig. 2.2. Cross section of a common wood rasp.

the curved side of the rasp should be used. When the surface to be formed is convex in both planes, it is possible to do some of the shaping with the curved side but most of the work should be done with the flat side.

Wood rasps are made with a number of grades of coarseness. Figure 2.3 shows photographs of portions of the flat surfaces of four different wood rasps magnified two times.

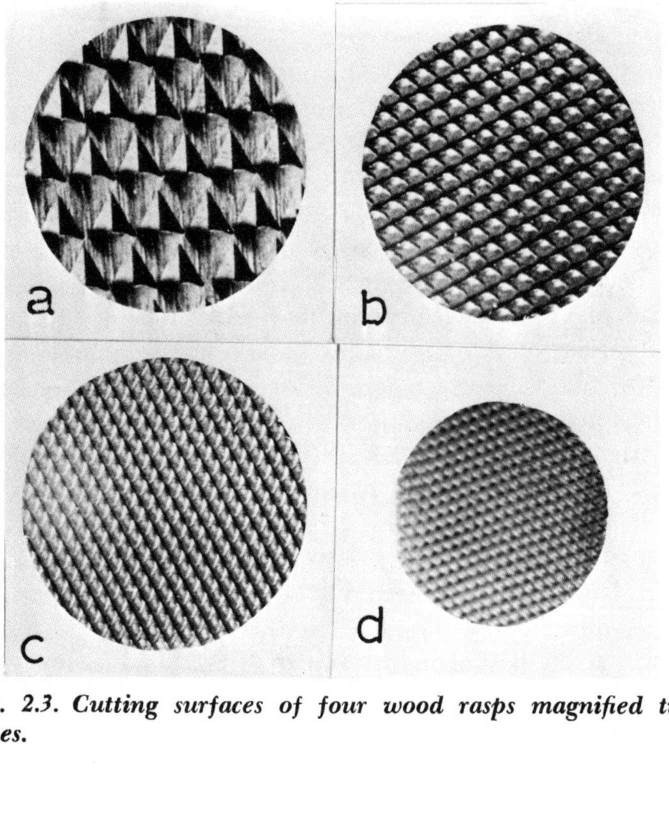

Fig. 2.3. Cutting surfaces of four wood rasps magnified two times.

The rasp that should be chosen for a given operation will depend on the amount of wood to be removed. The rasp is normally stroked across the grain. If it is stroked parallel to the grain of the wood, the rasp is not very effective because the cutting points will simply slide along the grain.

The points of the rasp tend to tear the wood, so the normal procedure is to use the coarse rasp to rough the surface down to a preliminary contour and then use successively finer rasps to approach the final contour. You should plan to leave some wood to be removed after the finest rasp has been used because, even the finest rasp will leave a rough surface. The coarsest rasp, *a* in Fig. 2.3, is seldom used, as it is difficult to use such a coarse rasp without damaging the piece.

We have many instances, in constructing furniture, where the end grain of a piece is finished. The surface left by the saw will not be smooth and it would require a great amount of labor to sand such a surface sufficiently to produce a desirable finish surface. Such an end grain can be finished with the finest rasp followed by finishing with a file which will be described in the next section.

The inexperienced amateur may have difficulty forming a flat surface with a rasp or file. The normal tendency is to form a rounded surface as indicated in Fig. 2.4 *a,* because of the tendency to rock the rasp while it is being stroked. Considerable practice is required to learn to stroke a rasp or file in a straight line to maintain a flat surface as in Fig. 2.4 *b*.

Occasionally an opening is to be formed in a piece such as the hand hole shown in Fig. 2.5 which might be made in the end of a tray. The hole can first be roughed out with a hand scroll saw or a jig saw, after holes are bored near each end. The inside of the hole should be properly shaped with rasps. Often, the radius of curvature of the curved

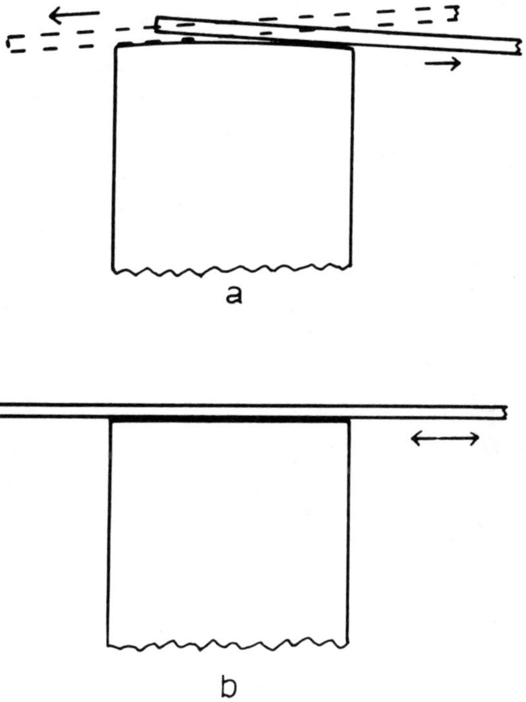

Fig. 2.4. Use of a rasp or file to form a flat surface on end grain. a *shows the rounded surface which is formed when the rasp or file is rocked when it is stroked.* b *shows the flat surface formed when the rasp or file is stroked without rocking.*

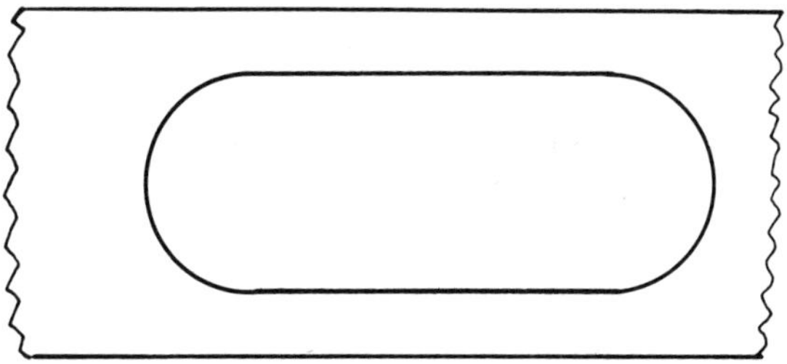

Fig. 2.5. Hand hole such as would be cut in the end of a tray.

side of the rasp will be too large to shape a small radius of curvature surface. There are, however, round rasps available, sometimes called rat tail rasps, which can be used for such an operation. A rasp tends to be self cleaning, but it is sometimes necessary to clean the surface of accumulated wood particles with a file cleaning brush. A fine rasp has more tendency to fill up with waste wood than a coarse rasp does.

2.4. Files

The action of a file is quite different from that of a rasp. A rasp has a surface designed to tear the wood and therefore is capable of removing the wood quite rapidly. The ridges on a file are like tiny planes which cross the surface of the file at an angle of about 65 degrees to the edge of the file. Since the cutting ridges on the file behave like planes, the file should normally be stroked parallel to the grain of the wood, although there are instances where the file is stroked perpendicular to the grain.

One important difference between the action of a plane and a cutting edge of a file is that the shaving produced by a plane can travel through the slot in the base and out above the plane. The shaving produced by a cutting edge on a file is trapped in the space between the cutting edges so that the file will fill up with waste wood after a few strokes. It is, therefore, necessary to clean the file frequently with a file cleaning brush. If the waste wood is allowed to become too tightly packed into the spaces between the cutting edges it may be difficult to dislodge it with the cleaning brush. When it is not possible to dislodge the waste wood with the cleaning brush, a special file cleaner can be made from a piece of soft aluminum. This should be made from a piece of sheet aluminum about 1/2 inch wide which can be pressed against the surface of the file at an angle of about 45 degrees and pushed parallel to the grooves on the file. The cutting edges on the file will cut grooves in the edge of the aluminum to form portions between these grooves which will scoop out the waste wood between the cutting edges.

When a piece of wood is shaped with rasps and smoothed, first with a coarse file and then with a fine file it is possible to produce a very fine finished surface. Many violin makers prefer a finish produced by a fine file to a sand paper finish.

2.5. Scrapers

The general purpose hand scraper is made from a piece of alloy steel about 1/32 inch thick and about 2 1/2 by 5 inches. To prepare the scraper for use it must be properly sharpened. There are five steps in properly sharpening a scraper. First, clamp the scraper in a vise and, holding a fine mill file perpendicular to the sides of the scraper, file the edge square and straight. The corners should then be rounded slightly so that they will not dig in when the scraper is used. Second, holding the scraper perpendicular to the surface of an oil stone, whet the edge by moving it back and forth parallel to its length. Third, lay the flat side of the scraper on the oil stone and move it back and forth until the burr is removed. This should be done on both sides. Fourth, using a polished, hard steel burnishing tool with the scraper lying flat on the edge of the bench and the burnishing tool held flat on the scraper, draw the edge with three or four firm strokes of the burnisher. Fifth, hold the burnishing tool as indicated in Fig. 2.6, where *A* is the burnishing tool and *B* is the scraper, stroke the tool the length of the blade with a firm stroke with the angle *a* at 90 degrees. Follow this with three or four strokes,

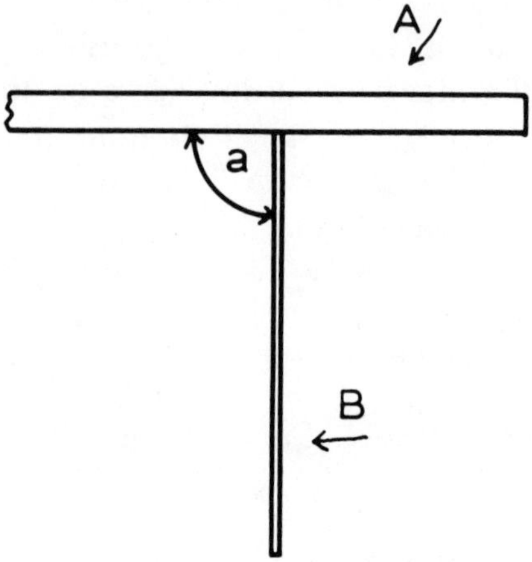

Fig. 2.6. Use of a burnishing tool to form the cutting burr on a scraper.* A *is the burnishing tool and* B *is the scraper.

tilting the burnisher slightly for each stroke until the last stroke is made at an angle of about 85 degrees. A small drop of oil should be applied to the burnisher.

The burnisher develops a fine burr along the edge of the blade which will cut a fine shaving as the scraper is pushed along the surface of the wood.

To use the scraper, it should be held in the two hands with the thumbs at *A* and *A'* in Fig. 2.7 and the fingers at

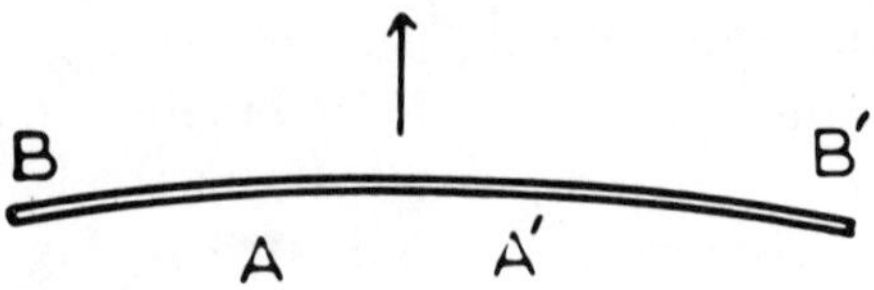

Fig. 2.7. Method of holding a scraper to slightly bow the blade. The thumbs are placed at* A *and* A' *and the fingers at* B *and* B'. *The arrow indicates the direction in which the blade is pushed.

B and *B'* so that the scraper blade can be very slightly bowed. It is then pushed in the direction of the arrows in Figs. 2.7 and 2.8, generating the shaving as indicated at *A* in Fig. 2.8.

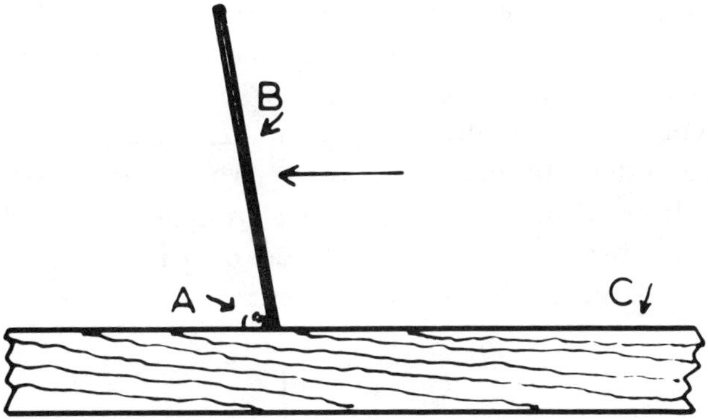

Fig. 2.8. View parallel to the scraper blade showing its action. B is the scraper blade, C is the wood surface and A is the shaving being produced. The wavy lines show the direction of the wood grain.

The scraper should never be pushed against the grain of the wood, as it would cause the ends of the grain to chip. Figure 2.8 shows the scraper being pushed in the proper direction relative to the grain. *B* is the scraper, *C* is the wood and the direction of the grain of the wood is indicated by the wavy lines.

General purpose scrapers can be used on flat and convex surfaces. Special curved scrapers are also used on concave surfaces and by bowing the general purpose type of scraper it can be used on concave surfaces if the curvature of the surface is not too great. Violin makers use special small curved scrapers for scraping the complex curved surfaces of the violin plates. These scrapers are usually considerably thinner than the straight cabinet scrapers used in most conventional furniture work.

2.6. Gouges

Gouges are made in a variety of sizes. They differ from chisels in that the end of the blade is curved. They are used for hollowing out depressions in a wood surface.

A gouge should always be kept very sharp. Since the cutting end is curved, it cannot be ground on a carborunbum wheel in the same manner as a straight blade such as a plane or chisel. The easiest method of grinding the bevel is to hold the blade on the steady rest *A* in Fig. 2.9 and

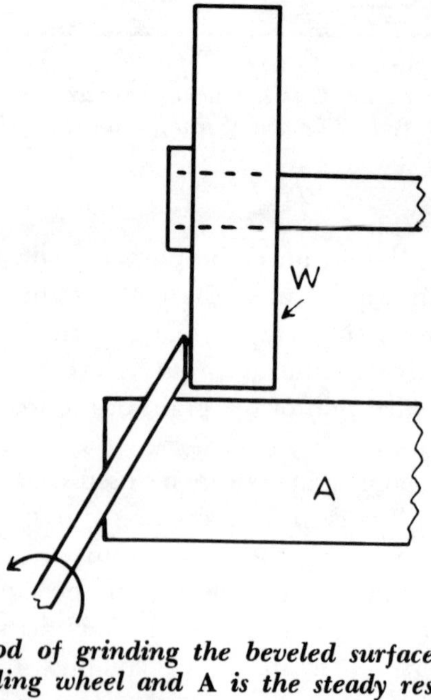

Fig. 2.9. Method of grinding the beveled surface on a gouge. W is the grinding wheel and A is the steady rest. The arrow shows the direction of rotation of the gouge in order to grind the entire surface.

grind the bevel on the side of the wheel *W*. The bevel should be about 1/4 inch. The blade should be rotated slowly in the direction of the arrow in Fig. 2.9 to form a uniform bevel like that shown in Fig. 2.10 which shows

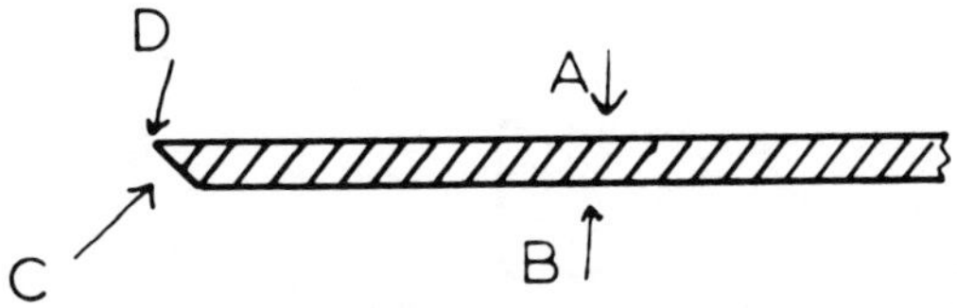

***Fig. 2.10. Longitudinal section of a gouge blade.* A *is the concave side of the blade,* B *is the convex side and* C *is the bevel. The burr formed during grinding and honing on the bevel surface is at* D.**

a longitudinal section of the blade. The bevel thus formed will not be hollow ground as the bevel on a chisel is which is ground on the circumference of the wheel. In Fig. 2.10, *A* is the concave side of the blade and *B* is the convex side. After the blade is sharpened on the grinding wheel, the surface *C* is honed on the concave side of a special curved oil stone, gradually rotating it so that all portions of the edge are uniformly honed. The grinding and honing will cause a burr to develop on the edge *D* which is the forward edge of the concave surface of the blade. If the gouge is large and has a large enough radius of curvature the burr can be removed by honing the concave side of the blade on the convex side of the curved oil stone. Small gouges can have this burr removed by honing them on a special wedge shaped stone like that shown in Fig. 2.11 where the two edges *A* and *B* are curved. The stone should be stroked parallel to the length of the blade while it is held very lightly against the surface. This honing should be continued until the burr is just removed. Too much honing can develop a burr on the other side of the edge. You can tell

*Fig. 2.11. Special stone for removing the burr formed on a gouge in grinding and honing. Edge **A** has a small radius of curvature and edge **B** has a larger radius of curvature.*

when the burr is removed by feeling the edge with your finger.

In using a gouge, it is held as indicated in Fig. 2.12 and it should be driven by tapping the end of the handle with

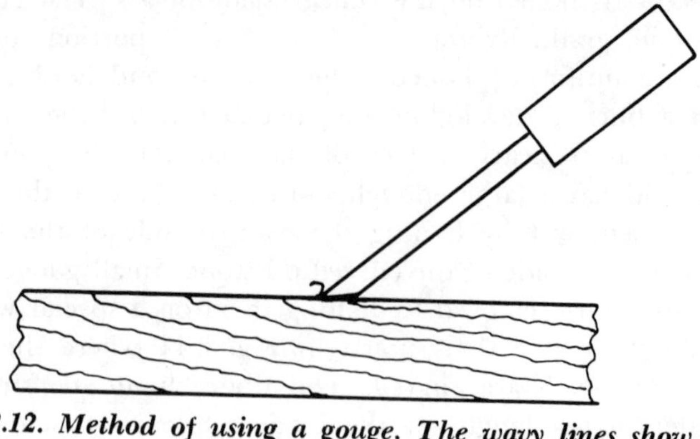

Fig. 2.12. Method of using a gouge. The wavy lines show the direction of the wood grain.

a mallet. There may be some instances when the gouge may be pushed with your hand. However, it is very difficult to control it unless it is driven with a mallet. In any case, never push the gouge toward your other hand, as such action is almost certain to result in injury.

When a gouge is used to carve out a depression, such as the depression in the seat of a windsor chair, the outline of the depression should be marked and the wood should be removed by working from the outline toward the center. The gouge should never be driven so that it cuts against the grain.

After a depression has been roughed out with a gouge it can be smoothed with a scraper before sanding.

I have found very few instances where the sanding attachment for a small hand drill can be useful because of its tendency to form circular sanding gouges. However, I have found that such a sander can be useful for the rough sanding of depressions. The sanding disc should be pressed very lightly on the surface and stroked from the edge of the depression toward the lowest point. The flexible rubber backing for the sanding disc allows it to follow the shape of the curved surface being formed. It is necessary to follow with hand sanding as the rotating sanding disc will be sanding across the grain as well as parallel to the grain and final hand sanding parallel to the grain will be necessary to remove the scratches.

2.7. Forming Very Deep Depressions

When very deep depressions are to be scooped out it is possible to reduce the amount of labor required with the gouges by boring out a series of closely spaced holes nearly to the bottom of the depression. The depth of the holes can be controlled by means of the stop on the drill press spindle. The wood between the holes can be easily roughed out with a gouge. Great care should, of course, be exercised to avoid drilling any of the holes beyond the desired depth.

3
Bending Wood

3.1. Introduction

Parts of furniture are often curved. In some instances, it is best to cut these curved parts from a solid piece but there are instances where it is best to bend the wood to the desired shape. A bent piece is stronger than one cut to shape and cutting the piece to shape is often wasteful of material.

When a piece of material is bent, as in Fig. 3.1, the material on the side *A* is compressed and that on the side *B* is stretched. Wood fibers can be compressed but they cannot be stretched appreciably without breaking. If the piece of material in Fig. 3.1 is wood, there will be very little stretching along the side *B* and most of the change in shape will take place as a result of compression of the fibers on the side *A*.

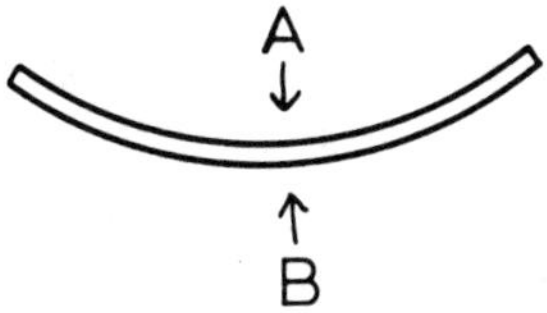

Fig. 3.1. An example of a bent piece of material.

Hardwoods such as maple, hickory, oak, elm and walnut can be bent quite easily. It is more difficult to bend cherry. Any wood which is to be bent should be carefully selected for straight grain parallel to the length of the piece.

3.2. Use of Bending Irons

In order to bend wood, it is necessary to soften the fibers with water or steam. This can be readily accomplished by soaking the wood and applying a hot iron to the surface to generate steam which can penetrate the surface of the wood. A bending iron should have a convex surface shaped like the concave surface to be generated on the wood. The iron should be heated to a temperature just below that which would char thin shavings. The wood should be thoroughly soaked in water and then forced gradually around the iron. As the wood is forced around the hot iron, the water in the surface will be changed to steam which will penetrate the wood softening the fibers so that they will compress. The wood should be held in place on the iron until it is dry.

3.3 Bending Wood on Improvised Forms

Amateurs usually do not have bending irons available. It is, however, possible to bend pieces of wood for furniture parts with wooden jigs or forms. These can be cut from plywood or solid planks to build up a form as wide as the piece to be bent. The layers to be used to build up the form can be cut to the proper shape with a band saw. The curved surfaces of the jig which will be in contact with the wood to be bent should be sanded smooth and coated with sealer. Figure 3.2 shows a jig constructed by the author for use in bending the sides for an Appalachian mountain dulcimer and Fig. 3.3 shows one used for bending the

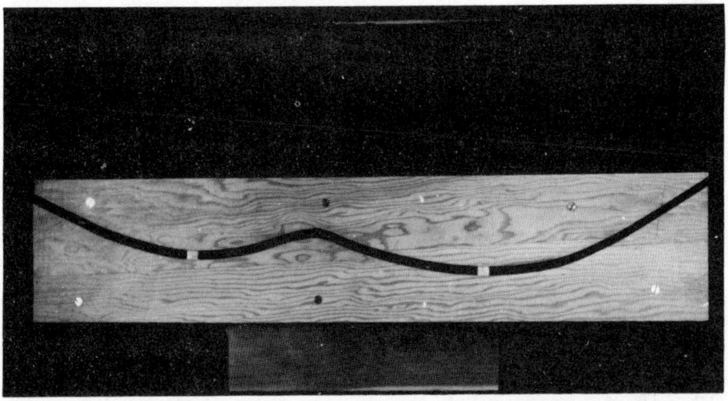

Fig. 3.2. A jig used for bending a side of a dulcimer.

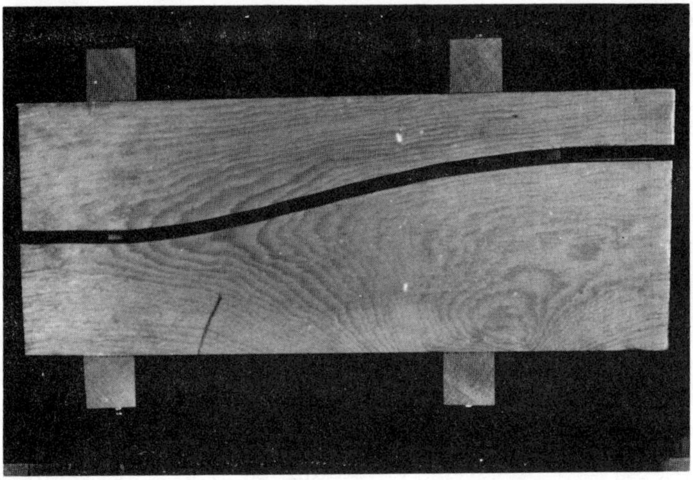

Fig. 3.3. A jig used for bending the back splat of a chair.

back splat for a Queen Anne chair.

In order to soften the wood it should be soaked in boiling water for about one hour. A wood such as cherry, which is difficult to bend, should be soaked in water at room temperature over night before soaking in the boiling water.

Immediately after removing the wood from the boiling water, it should be placed in the jig which should then be slowly clamped to force the wood to its proper shape. It is important to apply the clamps slowly in order to allow the fibers time to assume the desired shape. The wood should be left in the jig until it is throughly dry which will usually require several days.

3.4. Bending Laminations

Thin laminations can be bent with little or no soaking. The thinner the lamination, the smaller the radius of curvature of bend which can be produced. By stacking laminations with a film of resin glue between them and clamping the stack in a jig of the proper shape until the glue is dry, it is possible to form a laminated wood shape which will be very strong. All of the layers in such a structure should have the direction of the grain of the wood run in the same direction. The layers should not be arranged so that the wood will be bent across the grain.

It is possible to use thicker laminations if each lamination is soaked and bent in the jig as described in Section 3.3. When all of the laminations have been bent and left in the jig until dry, they can be assembled with glue between them and the entire assembly clamped in the jig until the glue has cured.

A layer of waxed paper should be placed between the assembly and the jig on each side to prevent the assembly from becoming attached to the jig with glue which may squeeze out when the jig is clamped.

A modification of the use of laminations for forming a bend on the end of a piece of lumber is illustrated in Fig. 3.4. The kerfs *A* are cut with a band saw which makes a

Fig. 3.4. Use of saw kerfs to laminate the end of a piece to be bent.

narrow cut. Layers of veneer with glue applied to their two sides are inserted in the kerfs and the end of the piece is clamped in a jig of the desired shape. This is a convenient means of bending the toe of a ski. After the glue has cured in the form, the piece can be shaped. The kerfs should not all be cut to the same depth, as indicated in Fig. 3.4.

4

Moldings

4.1. Introduction

Moldings have long been used to enhance the appearance of furniture. The first moldings were probably hand carved, but special planes were then developed which would accept especially shaped blades for cutting the various shaped cuts to produce the desired surface on the molding. These planes were also equipped with an adjustable edge guide to force the plane to make the molding cut at the proper distance from the edge.

With the availability of modern power tools, it is possible to make the same kinds of molding cuts with a power saw equipped with a molding head, a router, a shaper or even a drill press. The principle involved is the same as that with the molding cutting plane, so the shapes of the cutting edges of the cutter blades used on the power tools is the same as those used on the molding cutting planes in most instances.

4.2. Cove Moldings

A cove may be used as a part of a more complex molding, or it may constitute the entire molding. Figure 4.1 shows

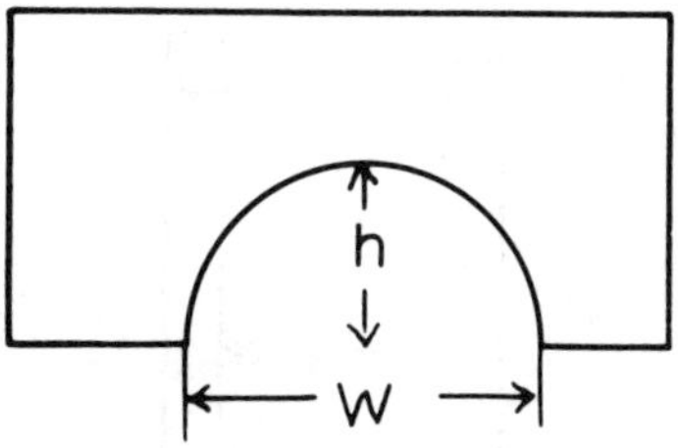

Fig. 4.1. Cross section of a cove cut on a flat surface.

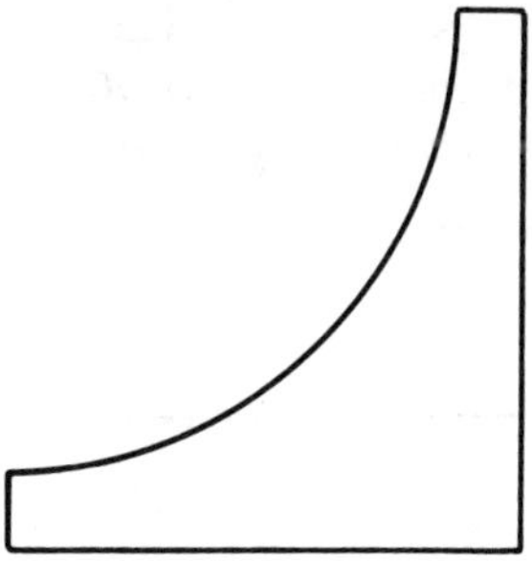

Fig. 4.2. Cross section of a cove cut on a diagonal surface.

a cross section of a typical cove. It may be cut in the flat side of a piece of lumber or it may be cut in a piece such as that in Fig. 4.2. The cove is designated by the width *W* and the height *h* in Fig. 4.1. The cove is a very simple molding to cut, as no special molding cutters are needed. It is cut directly with a power saw by guiding the workpiece through the saw at an angle.

To prepare to cut a cove, raise the saw above the saw table so that it will make a cut equal to the height *h*. Now, using some scrap lumber, make a frame like that in Fig. 4.3 with the sides parallel and separated so that the spacing between the inside edges is equal to *W* in Fig. 4.1. Place this frame over the saw as indicated in Fig. 4.4 and turn

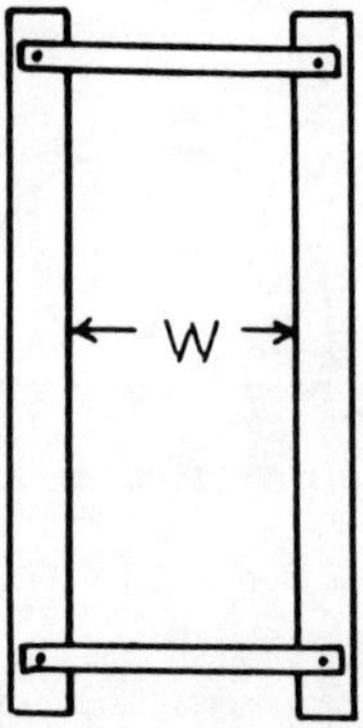

Fig. 4.3. Improvised frame for use in determining the angle at which the workpiece should be guided through the saw to cut a cove of width W.

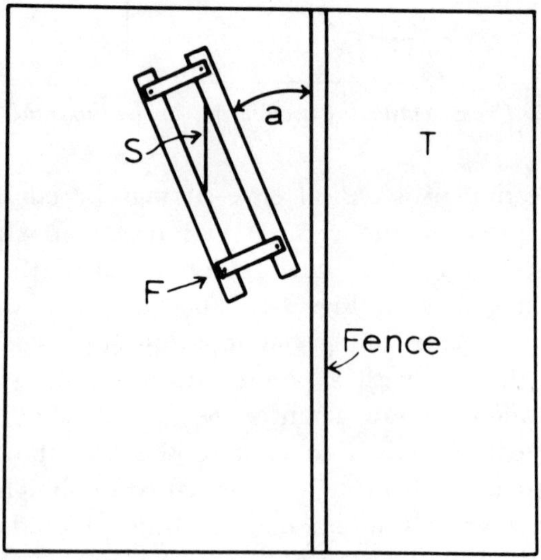

Fig. 4.4. Use of the frame shown in Fig. 4.3 to determine the angle at which the workpiece will be guided through the saw to cut a cove.

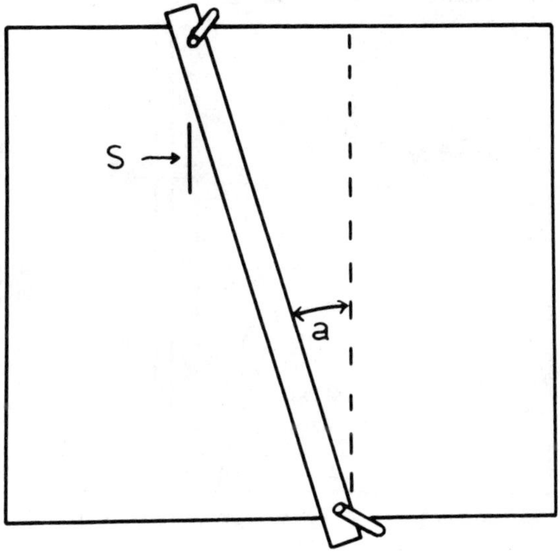

Fig. 4.5. An improvised temporary fence for use as a guide in cutting a cove.

it at an angle such that the inside edges just touch the saw teeth. In Fig. 4.4, *T* is the saw table, *S* is the saw and *F* is the frame. The angle *a* in Fig. 4.4 is the angle at which the workpiece must be guided through the saw. You can prepare a temporary fence by clamping a piece of lumber to the saw table as indicated in Fig. 4.5, where the temporary fence makes the angle *a* with the saw fence, or you can make a jig as indicated in Fig. 4.6 which can be set at the angle *a* and clamped to the saw fence in the proper position so that the workpiece on which the cove will be cut can be guided along the jig as the cove is cut. You can set the jig and the saw fence to cut the cove in the proper place by adjusting the spacing *d* by means of the adjustment of position of the saw fence or by moving the jig along the saw fence. When this adjustment has been made, you are ready to cut the cove.

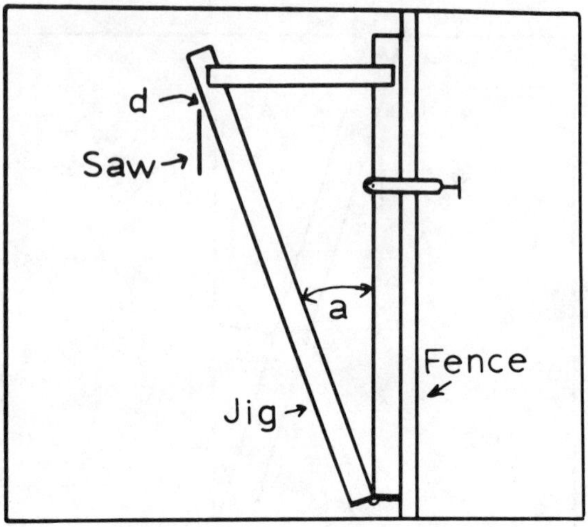

Fig. 4.6. Special jig for a fence for use as a guide in cutting a cove.

It is not possible to cut the entire depth of the cove in one cut. You can start by lowering the saw until it projects about 1/8 inch above the saw table and guide the workpiece through the saw using the temporary fence as a guide. After this first cut is made, check to determine if the center of the cut is at the center of the desired cove. It may be necessary to make a slight correction in the position of the saw fence. Now make successive cuts, raising the saw slightly for each cut until the cove is cut to the desired width. Usually the width *W* in Fig. 4.1 is more critical than the height *h,* so the saw is raised until the proper width is reached. It will be necessary to sand the cove surface after it is cut to remove the marks of the saw.

If the molding is composed of other molding cuts in addition to a cove, the cove should be cut first and the other molding cuts are made later.

4.3. Cutting Moldings on a Power Saw

It is possible to cut moldings on a power saw by replacing the saw blade with a molding head which can accept various shapes of molding cutters. Figure 4.7 shows a

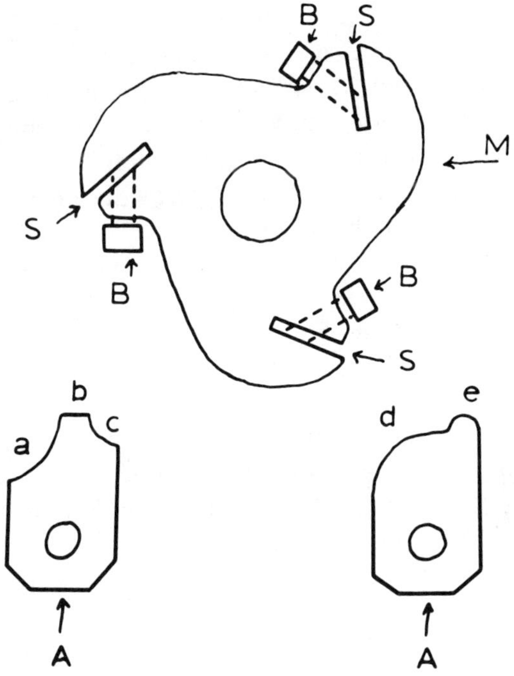

Fig. 4.7. A small molding cutter head for use on a saw with two typical molding cutters.

typical molding head. The slots in which the cutters are mounted are indicated at *S* and the bolts for locking the cutters in place are indicated at *B*. When the molding head is used, three identical cutters are mounted in the three slots *S*.

Two typical shapes of molding cutter are indicated at *A* and *A'* in Fig. 4.7. The cutter at *A* has cutting surfaces *a* and *c* which can cut convex surfaces of two different radii of curvature. The surface *b* can be used to cut a narrow slot. The cutter at *A'* has a cutting surface *d* for cutting a concave surface and a surface *e* for cutting a round bottomed slot. The surfaces *a, c* and *d* are usually used for cutting moldings on the edges of workpieces.

The usual molding cutters are about 1 inch wide, so a thick washer is supplied with the molding head which must be placed between the molding head and the saw frame to provide adequate clearance for the cutters.

The plate on the saw table through which the saw projects must be replaced by a special plate which has a slot wide enough to accommodate the molding cutters. If you do not have such a plate, it is usually possible to purchase one to fit your saw. However, if you cannot purchase the special plate to accommodate the cutters, you can purchase an extra plate for the saw and cut out the necessary area to accommodate the molding cutters. Do not attempt to use the cutters without a plate and do not modify the plate which you use with the saw blades. In either instance, the result can lead to serious injury.

A large number of shapes of molding cutters are available and complex moldings are made by making successive cuts with the various shapes of cutters. You can control the depth of cut with the cutter by means of the height adjustment of the saw arbor and the position of each particular cut is controlled by means of the saw fence.

Due to the fact that some of the cuts will need to be made with a part of the cutter under the fence, it will be necessary to make a wooden face for the fence like that shown in Fig. 4.8. The screws *S* are used to attach the wood face to the fence and the clearance *C* can be cut using

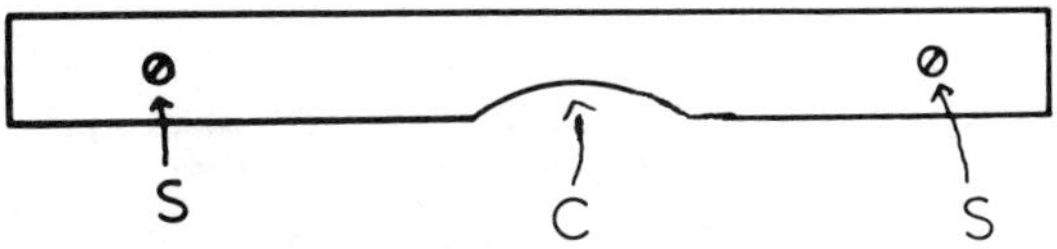

Fig. 4.8. Temporary wood face for a saw fence for use with the molding head.

straight knives in the molding head. The wood face for the fence should be made from a piece of hard wood, such as maple, at least 1 inch thick. Straight moldings are cut by guiding the piece of lumber along the fence to make the various cuts.

It is possible to cut moldings on curved pieces of lumber with the molding head on a saw. If the piece on which the molding is to be cut is circular, the arrangement shown in Fig. 4.9 can be used. The two triangles *T* are clamped in

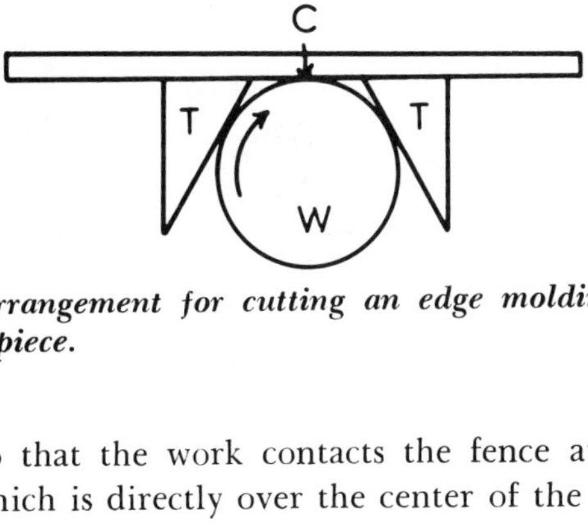

Fig. 4.9. Arrangement for cutting an edge molding on a circular workpiece.

position so that the work contacts the fence at the center point *C* which is directly over the center of the arbor shaft. The work is rotated so that it moves against the motion of the molding cutter blades.

If a molding is to be cut on a convex surface, which is not circular, the arrangement shown in Fig. 4.10 can be

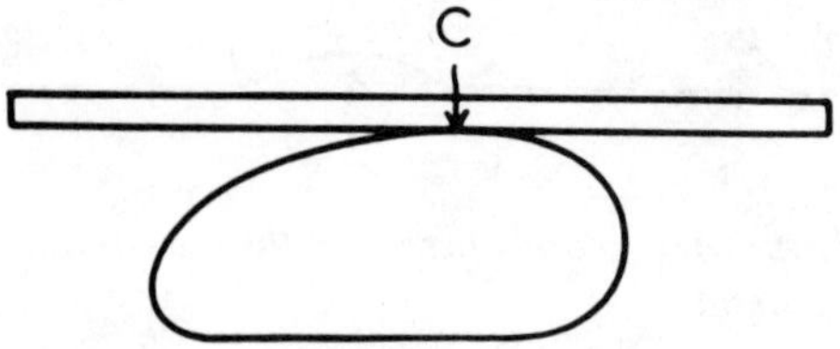

Fig. 4.10. Arrangement for cutting an edge molding on a convex curved workpiece.

used. *C* is again the center over the arbor shaft and the work is moved so that it maintains contact with the fence at *C*.

It is also possible to cut moldings on a concave surface, if the molding to be cut is not very deep and the radius of curvature of the surface is fairly large, with the arrangement shown in Fig. 4.11. The workpiece is moved so that

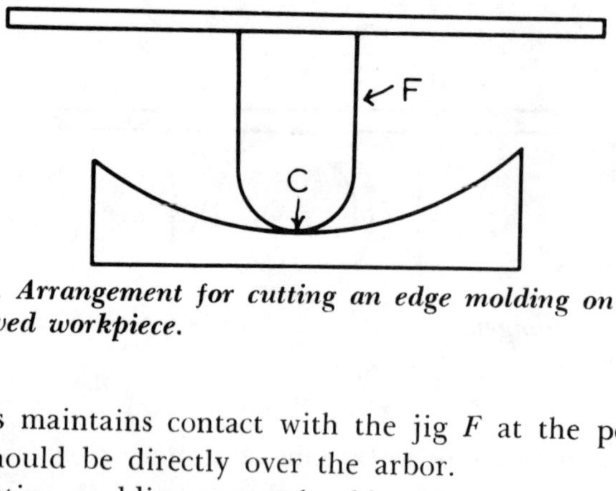

Fig. 4.11. Arrangement for cutting an edge molding on a concave curved workpiece.

it always maintains contact with the jig *F* at the point *C* which should be directly over the arbor.

In cutting moldings, you should seldom try to cut the full depth of the molding with a single pass over the cutter. A series of passes should be made with the saw arbor raised slightly between passes. The distance the saw arbor should be raised for each pass depends on the size of the cut and the nature of the wood being cut. If too deep a cut is attempted, there may be a tendency for the surface to chip so that considerable sanding will be required to obtain a smooth surface.

Wide moldings, made with several cuts using more than one shape of molding cutter, are often used around the tops of large pieces of furniture. These moldings are usually cut on the face of a piece of 3/4 inch or 7/8 inch lumber and the piece is usually mounted as indicated in Fig. 4.12

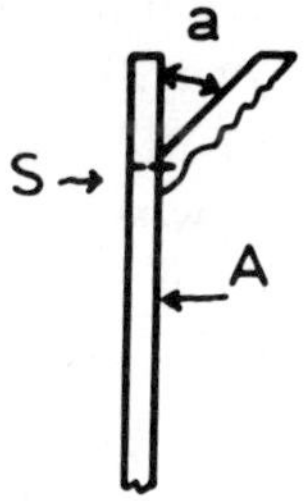

Fig. 4.12. Method of mounting a wide molding at the top of a large piece of furniture.

where the angle *a* is 45 degrees. The molding is attached to the surface *A* of the piece of furniture by means of the screws *S*. If the grain of the wood in the furniture and the molding runs in the same direction, glue can be used in addition to the screws. However, if the grain of the wood in the furniture is perpendicular to that of the molding, no glue should be used and the screw holes through the wall of the furniture should be slightly oversized to allow for the difference in contraction and expansion, with changes in relative humidity, between the furniture wall and the molding.

In order to cut the miters, where the molding on two adjacent sides join at the corners, the molding is attached to a straight piece of lumber in the same manner as it will be attached to the face of the piece of furniture in order to hold it in the proper orientation while the miter is being cut. When the molding is applied to the piece of furniture, the mitered surfaces should be glued together at the corners.

The molding cutters which are used in the molding head are usually made of high speed steel and will hold an edge for a considerable time. When they need to be sharpened, they can be honed on a flat oil stone by placing the shiny side of the cutter on the stone so that the entire surface can be honed. A very dull cutter can be ground on the bevel edge but this is usually not practical for an amateur since all three of the cutters must be ground exactly the same, which is difficult without a special grinding jig for that particular style of cutter. Since these cutters are quite inexpensive, it is better to replace them when they become worn so that they cannot be satisfactorily honed on the flat surface.

4.4. The Shaper

A shaper has a vertical arbor so that the cutters rotate in thc horizontal plane. Although nearly any edge molding can be cut on either the shaper or the saw with a molding head, the shaper is more effective for cutting moldings on curved pieces. Few amateurs will invest in a shaper since it will have limited usefulness in an amateur shop.

4.5. The Drill Press as a Molding Cutter

Many drill presses can utilize a molding attachment which can be substituted for the chuck. The arrangement is like a shaper upside down. Since the cutters operate on the end of the drill press spindle, it is necessary to take rather thin cuts to avoid applying too great a side force on the spindle. Such an arrangement is quite effective. I have cut many moldings on my drill press. (Fig. 7.16) It simply takes longer to do the job than it would with a shaper.

4.6. The Power Router as a Molding Cutter

The power router is a hand power tool of many uses. One of its possible uses is in cutting moldings. The power router consists of a motor of approximately one horsepower mounted in a frame with the shaft vertical and having a chuck at the bottom end to hold the arbors of the various cutter bits. The subbase of the router frame consists of a phenolic disc about 6 inches in diameter with an opening in the center throughwhich the cutter bits project. The depth of projection of the bits below the subbase can be controlled and a scale can be read to measure the depth of cut to 1/64 inch. The router is held so that the phenolic subbase slides over the workpiece.

When a molding is to be cut on the edge of a workpiece, a cutter bit which has a pilot at its bottom end is used so that the pilot can guide the cutter bit along the edge of the workpiece. Such an edge molding can be cut equally well on straight, concave or convex surfaces. A number of shapes of cutter bits are available so that nearly any desired shape of edge molding can be produced.

An adjustable edge guide is also available for use with the router. The edge guide permits the router cutter bit to be moved parallel to the edge of the workpiece at any desired distance from the edge. The cutter bits used to cut over the body of the workpiece do not have pilots. Three common types of cutter bits used are straight bits, veining bits and V-grooving bits. The straight bits have a flat end and, therefore, cut a flat bottomed groove with straight sides and are available in a variety of sizes. The veining bits are similar to the straight bits except that they have a round bottom. Veining bits also are available in a variety of sizes. V-grooving bits have a pointed end so that they cut a V-shaped groove.

By means of the adjustments of the edge guide and the depth of cut and with the choice of sizes and shapes of cutter bits, it is possible to produce nearly any desired molding pattern.

When moldings are to be cut on small workpieces, it is difficult, and sometimes impossible, to handle the router on top of the workpiece. You can convert your router to a simple shaper to deal with this problem. Cut a piece of 1/4 inch hardboard about 12 inches square, drill a hole in the center the same size as the hole in the center of the router subbase and drill and countersink screw holes corresponding to the screw holes for mounting the subbase on the router.

Trace the outline of the 12 x12 inch hardboard on a piece of 3/4 inch plywood or chipboard about 2 x 3 feet and cut an opening in this board 11 x 11 inches, leaving a 1/2 inch margin between the edges of the opening and the tracing of the 12 x 12 inch hardboard. This margin must then be countersunk so that when the hardboard is in place it will be accurately flush with the surface of the large board. Attach the hardboard with countersunk screws at the corners.

The router can now be mounted under the hardboard by first removing the subbase from the router and attaching it to the hardboard with the subbase screws. Edge moldings are cut in the same manner as in normal use of the router except that the router is now upside down and the workpiece is moved instead of the router. For other kinds of moldings, the router edge guide cannot be used, so you must construct a fence which can be made from a 1 x 3 inch board pivoted near one end of the board on which the router is mounted so that clearance between the fence and the cutter can be varied. The fence can be locked in place at the other end by means of a C clamp.

It is usually not desirable to mount this improvised shaper on permanent legs as it would take up considerable space in the shop. I have found a convenient arrangement by placing one end on the saw table, securing it with C clamps, and the other end on the fence of the jointer.

5

Furniture Legs

5.1. Introduction

Nearly all furniture legs are turned over some portion of their length. Many, however, require other operations, some in addition to turning. The turning operation is described in my *Amateur Furniture Construction,* Section 4.1.2.

Some types of legs, such as the ball and claw, require hand carving to produce the desired shape. The Cabriole or Queen Anne legs may be partially turned and roughly shaped with a band saw or a hand scroll saw and the final shaping is done by removal of wood with rasps and, in some instances, carving tools. Spiral turned legs can be cut on a saw, since the turning is essentially a spiral cut cove.

5.2. Queen Anne or Cabriole Legs

The process of forming simple Queen Anne legs was described in *Amateur Furniture Construction,* Section 4.1.3. There are some instances where such legs are more complex, particularly when they are used on chairs. Figure 5.1 shows a leg for a Queen Anne side chair and Fig. 5.2 shows a cross section of the leg at D–D in Fig. 5.1. If this was a simple Cabriole leg, the cross section would be as in Fig. 5.3. The ridges at A in Figs. 5.1 and 5.2 are formed by

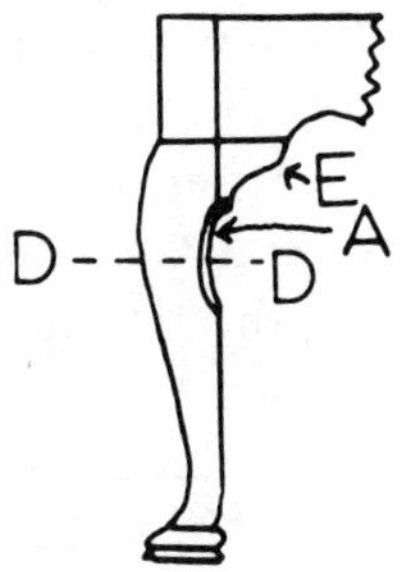

Fig. 5.1. Shape of a special cabriole leg for a Queen Anne chair.

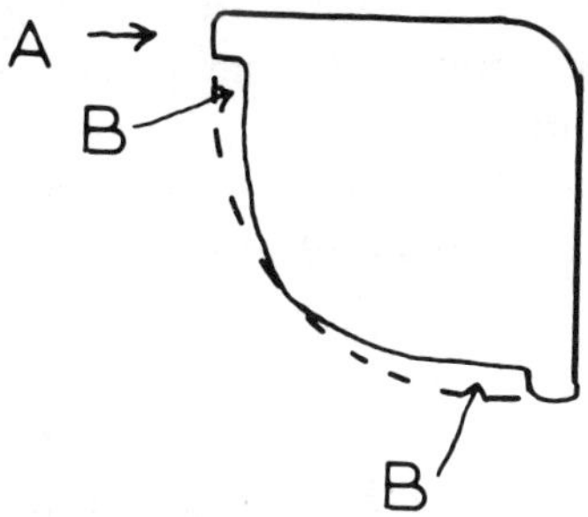

Fig. 5.2. Cross section of the leg shown in Fig. 5.1.

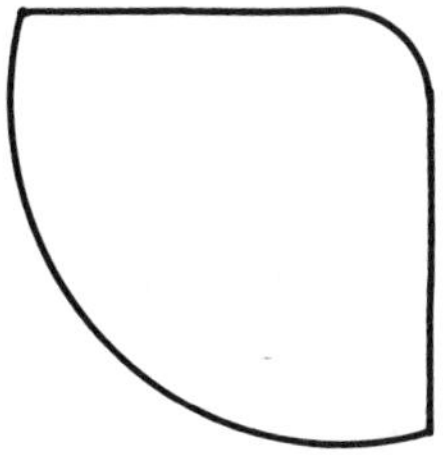

Fig. 5.3. Cross section of a simple cabriole leg.

carving the wood away in the regions B in Fig. 5.2 after the contour shown in Fig. 5.3 has been formed.

The method that I have used to form this type of leg is to form the leg in the shape shown in Fig. 5.3 and then trace the outline of the raised portion A in Figs. 5.1 and 5.2 with a marking gauge. A cut is then made with a sharp wood carving knife along the line marked with the marking gauge and the wood is then cut away up to this cut with a chisel. This process is repeated until a raised ridge of the desired height is formed. The contour of the new surface on the side of the leg, thus formed, is blended into the entire contour of the leg so that all changes in curvature are graceful.

Since the final shape of the leg is determined by your eye, all of the legs for a particular piece of furniture should be fabricated at the same time so that they can be formed to a similar shape. The absolute shape of the legs can vary somewhat from one piece of furniture to another but all of the legs for a given piece should be quite accurately similar.

When such a leg with the raised ridges is used, separate ears, like that shown at E in Fig. 5.1 must be made and glued in place after the rails are glued to the legs. Figure 5.4 shows the shape of one of these ears where it joins with the leg. The ridge A in Fig. 5.4 is made to form a continua-

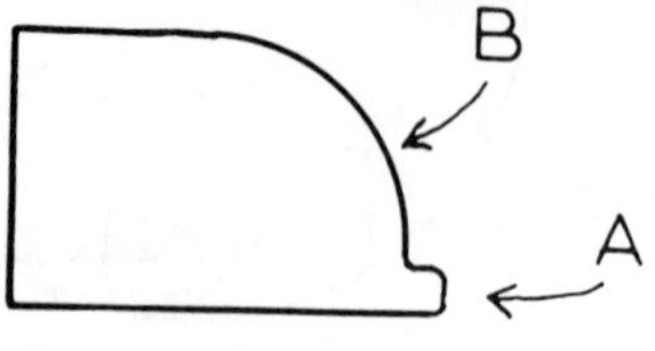

Fig. 5.4. Cross section of the special ear used with the leg shown in Fig. 5.1.

tion of the corresponding ridge A in Fig. 5.1 on the leg. These ears must be carved by hand so that the surface B in Fig. 5.4 matches the contour of the leg. The process of forming the ridge *A* in Fig. 5.4 is similar to that of forming the corresponding ridge on the leg.

There are some instances where ears, such as those shown at *E* in Fig. 5.1 are used with legs which do not have the

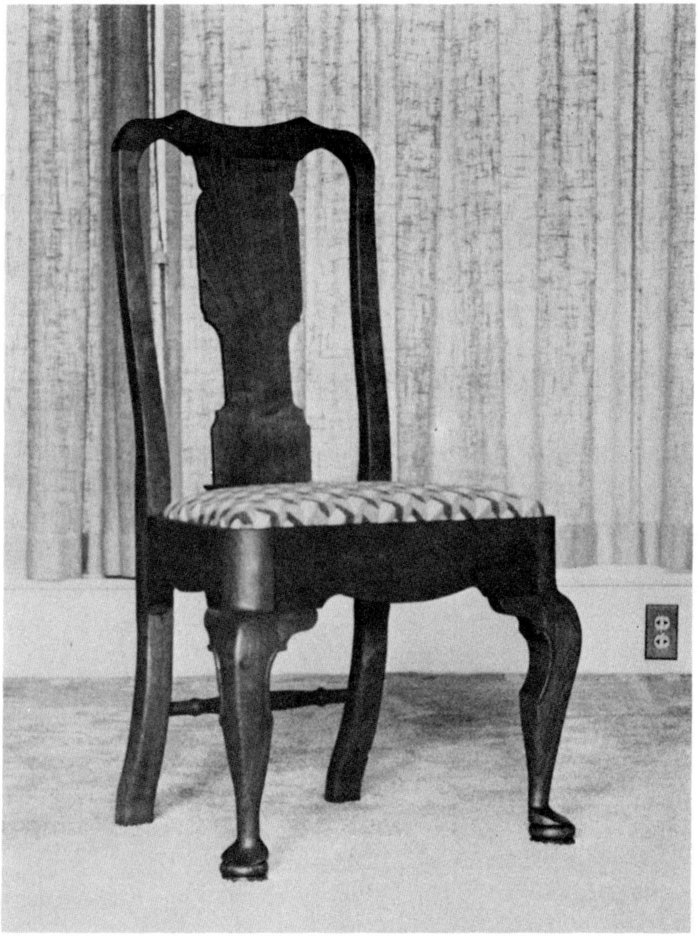

Fig. 5.5. A Queen Anne side chair.

raised ridge. Such ears will not have a raised ridge and they should simply be shaped to conform to the shape of the top of the leg. The raised ridges are most often used on chair legs while the legs without ridges, whether or not the separate ears are used, are most often used on tables.

Figure 5.5 is a photograph of a Queen Anne side chair, made by the author, with front legs similar to that shown in Fig. 5.1. This chair is similar to one in the Governor's mansion in Williamsburg except that the one in Williamsburg has a flat wooden seat and the chair in Fig. 5.5 has a padded seat covered with needlepoint.

The back corners of the legs must be cut away to accommodate the seat. The rails have a 1/4 inch rabbet cut to the depth of the seat and the legs must be cut away to the depth of the rabbets in the rails as indicated by the crosshatched portion in Fig. 5.6.

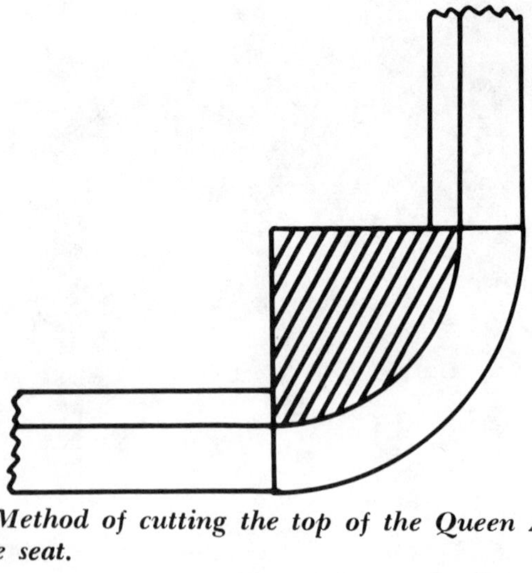

Fig. 5.6. Method of cutting the top of the Queen Anne leg to accept the seat.

5.3. Fluted Legs

Fluted legs are often used, especially on Sheraton tables. In some instances, the portion on which the fluting is applied has a constant taper from the top to bottom while in others, the fluted portion has a maximum diameter about 1/3 of the way from the top and gently tapers toward both the top and bottom. The leg must be turned to the desired shape before the fluting is done.

The fluting can be done with hand carving tools. To do this, the circumferential positions of the flutes is laid out using a pair of dividers. A line, parallel to the axis of the leg must be drawn from top to bottom of the fluted portion at the position of the maximum depth of cut between each of the flutes. Figure 5.7 is a cross section of the fluted portion of a leg and Fig. 5.8 shows the cutting end of a hand carving tool of the desired shape to carve the flutes. The

Fig. 5.7. Cross section of a fluted leg.

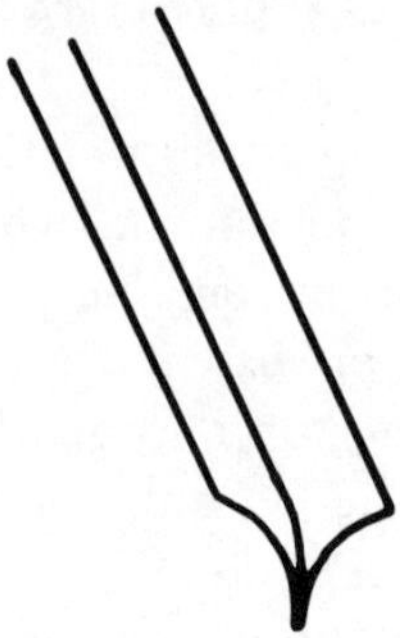

Fig. 5.8. Special carving tool for hand carving the flutes on a furniture leg.

carving should be worked from the region of largest radius on the leg toward regions of smaller radius to minimize danger of chipping. The carving tool should be driven by gently tapping with a mallet, first cutting a shallow groove the length of the flutes and then increasing the depth by successive passes until the required depth is attained. Do not attempt to carve the flutes by pushing the carving tool by hand as you cannot adequately control it. The leg must be firmly supported while the carving is being done.

If you have a turning lathe with a micrometer on the cross feed, it is possible to cut the flutes on the lathe. The position of the grooves between the flutes is laid off in the same manner as for hand carving except that it is not necessary to draw the lines the length of the flutes. In a set of legs that I made for a Sheraton table, the shape of the fluted portion is similar to Fig. 5.9. The maximum diameter is at A. By means of the micrometer on the cross feed of the lathe, measurements were made to locate the successive positions B_1, B_2, B_3 etc., where the radius decreases from the previous radius by 10/1000 inch.

A 60 degree thread cutting tool was set up in the tool

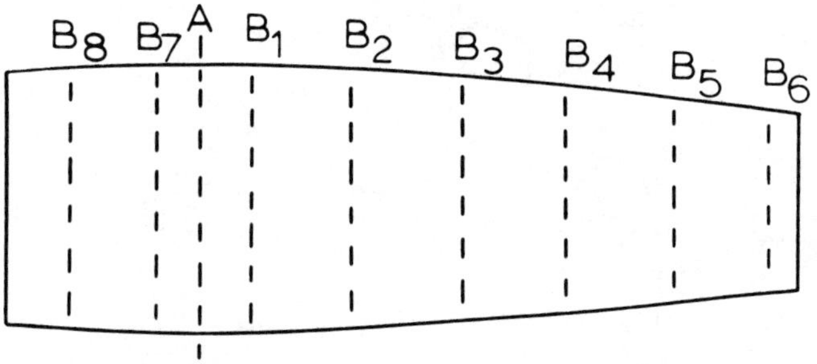

Fig. 5.9. Shape of the turning on which flutes are to be cut for a Sheraton table leg.

holder on the lathe with the tool positioned in the tool holder so that the 60 degree angle was in the vertical plane and the cutting surface was toward the right. The point of the tool was at dead center. The headstock was turned until one of the marked groove positions was directly under the point of the tool and locked so that it could not turn. The tool was then advanced until it just made contact with the leg at the position A in Fig. 5.9 and the tool carriage was then moved to the extreme left, the tool was advanced about 15/1000 inch and the carriage was driven by hand to the right. This caused a groove to be cut which varied over its length but was 15/1000 inch deep at A. Successive cuts were made, advancing the tool 15/1000 inch each time until a total of 10 cuts were made, which would reach a depth of 150/1000 inch at A. The tool was then moved to position B_1 and advanced 10/1000 inch and the carriage was moved to the right. It was then moved to B_2, advanced another 10/1000 inch and moved to the right again. This process was repeated at B_3, B_4 etc., until the right end of the fluting was reached.

The tool was then removed from the tool holder and rotated 180 degrees and the series of cuts were made start-

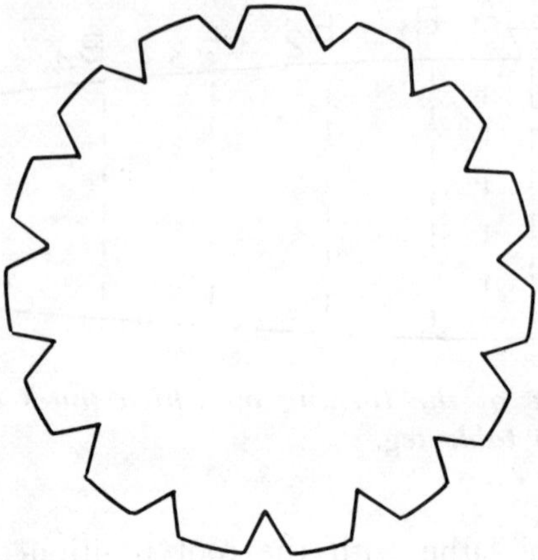

Fig. 5.10. Preliminary lathe cuts on a fluted leg.

ing at B_7, B_8 etc., until the groove was 150/1000 inch deep over the entire length of the groove.

The same procedure was repeated for each of the grooves and when completed the shape of the leg was like Fig. 5.10. The flutes were then rounded by sanding until they reached the shape shown in Fig. 5.7. Figure 4.15 in *Amateur Furniture Construction* shows a Sheraton table with the legs constructed as described above.

Figure 5.11 is a photograph showing a finished leg on the table with one which has the V-grooves cut on the lathe but has not had the flutes sanded to shape.

It will be possible to cut the flutes to the final shape by the above method if a special tool is ground having a shape like Fig. 5.12. This will avoid the necessity of sanding off the square corners of the flutes in Fig. 5.10. This will save some time if several fluted legs are to be made.

If a fluted leg with a straight taper is to be made, the entire depth of the groove between flutes can be cut with

Fig. 5.11. A finished fluted leg beside one with the V-grooves cut before the corners are sanded off.

Fig. 5.12. Special tool for cutting flutes on a lathe.

a single series of passes of the tool if the foot of the leg is mounted in the tail-stock of the lathe and the tail-stock is offset as it would be for turning a taper so the depth of cut will be the same over the entire length of the flutes on each pass of the tool.

5.4. Spiral Turned Legs

A spiral can be turned on a leg with a power saw. Although such a turning can be done on a lathe, it is a slow process and requires a lathe with an exceptionally low screw pitch.

To cut the spiral on a saw, a long wooden fence is attached to the saw miter by means of screws. The miter is set at about 75 degrees and it is clamped in position on the saw table as indicated in Fig. 5.13 so that the leg which has been turned round in the lathe will be directly over the

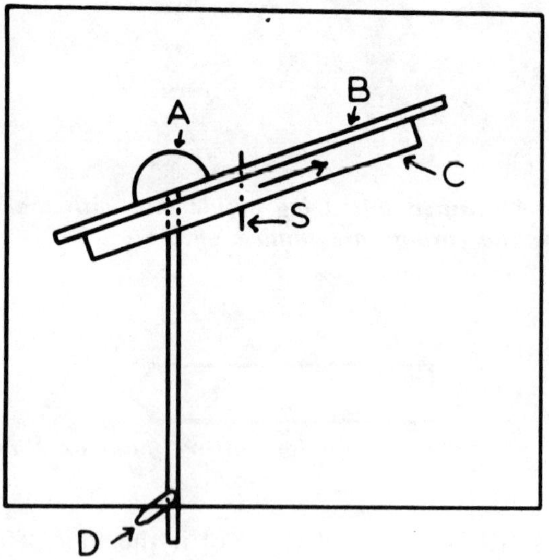

Fig. 5.13. Arrangement for cutting a guide spiral for a spiral turned leg.

saw arbor. In Fig. 5.13, A is the miter, B is the wooden fence attached to the miter, C is the leg to be turned, D is a C clamp to hold the miter in position and S is the saw which should be raised to make a cut about 3/16 inch deep. A stiff saw blade, such as a carbide tipped saw, should be used. As the leg is gradually pushed along the fence in the direction of the arrow, it will both turn and feed itself so that a nearly perfect spiral groove will be cut.

After the spiral groove is cut over the portion of the leg to be turned, the miter should be turned to a position about 60 degrees on the opposite side and a guide pin, which will fit the groove cut by the saw, is mounted in the face of the fence as indicated in Fig. 5.14, where T is the saw table, B is the fence, C is the piece to be turned and P is the guide pin.

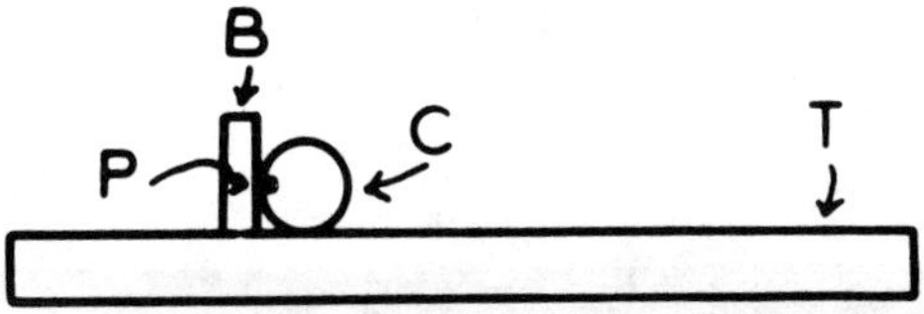

Fig. 5.14. Arrangement of the guide pin for cutting the spiral cove on a saw.

The molding head should now be put on the saw and a set of cutters similar to the one at A in Fig. 4.7 should be mounted in the molding head. The pin P should be located so that the groove cut by the saw will be directly over the molding cutter.

With the pin acting as a guide, the workpiece will be fed to the cutter which will cut a spiral cove. After the spiral cove is cut, the space between coves will have square corners. These corners can be rounded by mounting the leg in a lathe and rounding them with a rasp. The cove can then be sanded smooth in the lathe with a piece of sandpaper wrapped around a dowel pin. Any additional turning on the leg should be done after the spiral cove is completed.

The piece on which the spiral turning is to be cut should be quite smooth and the fence should be smooth. When the initial spiral cut is made, the leg should be gently turned against the fence with the fingers to help to overcome the friction of the leg against the fence. Before attempting to spiral turn a leg, you should first do some experimental samples; first to develop your technique so that you can make a satisfactory spiral cut with a uniform pitch over the entire length and then practice cutting the cove. If the spiral groove is satisfactory, it is relatively easy to make the cove cut. It is particularly difficult to do a spiral turning on soft wood. I have never had occasion to construct a piece of furniture with spiral turned legs, however, Fig. 5.15 shows my first attempt to turn a spiral on the saw. Note that the pitch of the spiral varies somewhat

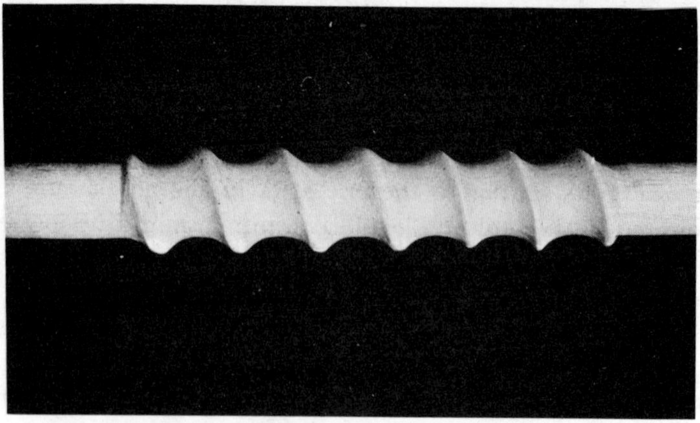

Fig. 5.15. A sample spiral turning.

over its length, probably due to the fact that this sample was made with white pine lumber.

5.5. Back Legs for Chairs

Most furniture, except chairs, require all of the legs to be identical. Chairs, generally, have different kinds of legs at the back than at the front. Usually the back legs of a chair extend to form the support for the back of the chair and the back legs are shaped approximately like that in Fig. 5.16. In some instances, the cross section of the leg is rectangular and should be cut out of a solid piece of stock with a band saw. The final detailed shaping is done with rasps. If a turned leg is to be shaped like Fig. 5.16, it will

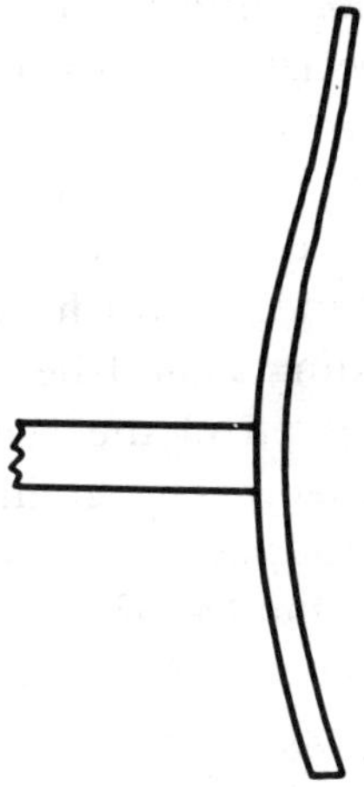

Fig. 5.16. General shape of the back legs for a chair.

be necessary to turn it as a straight piece and bend it after it has been turned. Methods of bending wood are described in Chapter 3.

6

Veneer and Inlay

6.1. Introduction

Veneer offers an opportunity to cover a surface with rare woods or wood of special grain such as crotch veneer and burl veneer.

Veneer stock is normally 1/28 inch thick. It can be applied directly to the surface to be covered or it can be applied over a layer of crossbanding which is a soft yellow poplar veneer. The crossbanding should be applied with its grain perpendicular to the grain of the veneer and the grain of the backing wood surface. The grain of the finish veneer will then be parallel to that of the backing wood.

There are many examples of fine old furniture which are veneered. By use of veneer it is possible to produce furniture with special grain surfaces which would be difficult to produce with solid lumber.

Some veneer is formed by shaving a thin layer of wood from a log as it is rotated in a large lathe. However, the finest veneers are formed by shaving slices from a flat piece of timber. Such veneers will have widths determined by the width of the piece of timber which is sliced.

6.2. Application of Veneer

A surface to which veneer is to be applied should be smooth and, if it is curved, the curvature should be gradual enough so that the veneer can be made to follow it. It is very important that the veneer make intimate contact with the surface without any trapped air bubbles as the air bubbles will eventually cause the veneer to blister.

The glue used to attach veneer must be non staining, as the veneer is very thin, so glue which will soak through and stain the surface will produce a mottled effect when the surface is finished. Before contact cement was available, the problem of clamping was difficult because the entire surface of the veneer would have to be pressed against the backing wood and held until the glue dried. When contact cement is used, both of the surfaces to be cemented together must be coated with the cement which is then allowed to dry until it is not sticky when touched with the fingers. The surfaces will then adhere when they are pressed together. The contact cement will not cause staining of the veneer as it does not soak through the veneer.

When contact cement is used to attach veneer to a backing wood, the back of the veneer sheet is coated with the cement by spreading it with a brush and the surface of the backing wood is coated in the same manner. When the cement is sufficiently dry, the veneer is applied and firmly rolled with a veneer roller or even a common rolling pin. The brush used to apply the cement can be cleaned with contact cement thinner.

Great care must be exercised to be certain that the veneer is applied exactly where it is wanted, as it is impossible to separate it from the backing wood once contact has been made. A good method of insuring that the veneer is properly oriented before it is allowed to contact the backing wood is to place a sheet of brown wrapping paper between the surfaces and, while the veneer is held in the proper position, the paper is gently pulled out from between the surfaces. The cement will not stick to the paper as it will stick only to another surface which has been coated with the cement.

Whenever possible, it is desirable to cut the veneer large enough to extend slightly beyond the edges so that it can be trimmed after the cement has had an opportunity to cure. A very sharp wood carving knife or a special veneer saw may be used for trimming the veneer as indicated in Fig. 6.1, where *A* is the veneered surface and *K* is the trim-

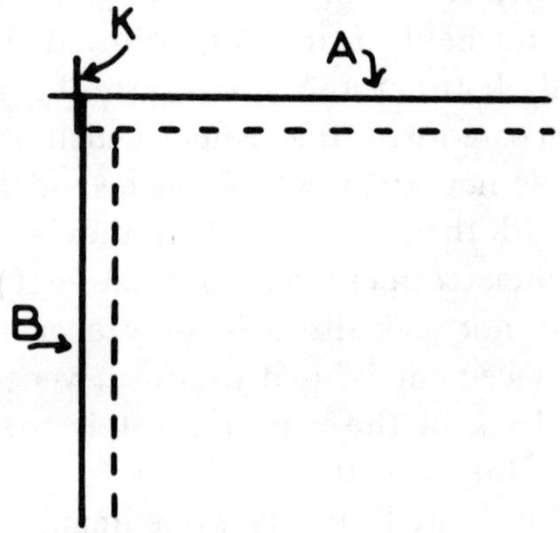

Fig. 6.1. Method of trimming veneer after it has been cemented to a surface.

ming knife or veneer saw. The veneer should be cut slightly beyond the surface *B* so that it can be sanded back flush with the surface *B*. If veneer is to be applied to the surface *B,* it will overlap the end of the veneer on surface *A*. In deciding the order in which surfaces are to be covered, it is best to leave the top until last so that its veneer will overlap the ends of the veneer on the sides.

When using contact cement, work in a well ventilated area, keep open flames away from the work area and keep the container closed except when cement is being used. The cement solvent is very volatile and inflammable. Be certain to read the directions on the cement container, as the specific instructions will vary somewhat from one brand to another.

The veneer stock should be handled carefully to avoid scratches or dents as it is not possible to do much sanding of the veneer surface because of the danger of sanding through the thin layer of the veneer.

It is possible to produce very sophisticated patterns with veneers. Anyone wishing to produce such complex patterns with veneer should consult a specialized book on veneering such as *Veneering Made Easy* by Albert Constantine, Jr., which can be purchased from Albert Constantine and Son, Inc., 2050 Eastchester Road, Bronx, N. Y. 10461.

There are some instances where it is not possible to prepare a suitable surface for standard thin veneer. For example, when I constructed a Sheraton banquet table which had curved ends like Fig. 6.2, it was not possible for me to pre-

Fig. 6.2. Method of forming the curved ends of a banquet table to receive a thick veneer.

pare the surface *A*, with the tools I had available, so that it would be perfect enough to accept thin veneer stock without danger of trapping air bubbles which would cause the veneer to blister. I was advised by a professional cabinetmaker to cut stock 1/8 inch thick with the saw, soak it in water and bend it to the desired shape and then glue this stock to the surface of the frame *B* in Fig. 6.2 which was built up of layers of white pine lumber and sawed to shape on a band saw. The fact that this thick veneer did not make contact at every point on the backing surface was not important as it would be impossible for an air bubble to cause a blister on 1/8 inch thick material. The special procedures for cutting such thin sheets on a power saw will be described in Section 8.4.

6.3. Crossbanding

Crossbanding is a veneer stock usually of soft yellow poplar which is often applied between the backing wood and the finish veneer. The crossbanding is applied with its grain perpendicular to that of the backing wood and the finish veneer is applied with its grain perpendicular to that of the crossbanding.

Crossbanding should always be used under crotch veneers and burls. It is available in 1/28 inch and 1/20 inch thicknesses and is applied in the same manner as the finish veneer. In any instance where the direction of the grain of the finish veneer should be the same as that of the backing lumber, it is advisable to use crossbanding.

6.4. Inlay

Inlay of a contrasting wood is often used as a means of decorating furniture. The inlay may be in the form of a complicated pattern or it may be applied as a line around a table top or around the edges of a table leg such as that shown in Fig. 6.3. Usually a white wood, such as maple, is

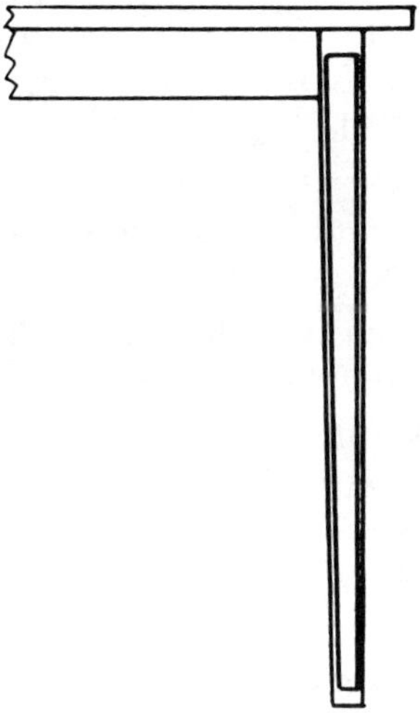

Fig. 6.3. Inlay at the edges of a square table leg.

used for inlay on a dark wood, such as walnut, cherry or mahogany. Figure 4.1 in *Amateur Furniture Construction* shows an example of maple inlay on walnut.

The inlay is usually about 1/20 to 1/16 inch thick and it is glued into a groove cut with a small flat bottomed router bit. For a line inlay the width will be determined by the diameter of the router bit. Usually widths of 1/20 to 1/16 inch are used.

When the inlay is in the form of a straight line, the groove can be cut with a hand router, using the edge guide. The bit should be set so that it will cut a groove at a depth slightly less than the thickness of the inlay stock so that after the inlay has been glued in place it can be sanded down flush with the surrounding wood.

If you do not have a hand router, you can do the job with the router bit in a drill press. In this case, the position of the bit will be fixed and the workpiece must be moved. For straight lines, a guide can be clamped to the drill press table, the spindle is lowered until the bit cuts to the proper depth and clamped in that position and the workpiece is moved along the guide.

For complex patterns of inlay, the pattern should be drawn on the wood and the groove is then cut by following the pattern with the router bit in the router or, if the router bit is mounted in a drill press chuck, the workpiece is moved so that the bit will follow the line. The thin narrow inlay stock can be bent dry around a considerable curvature, however, if the bends are too sharp for the inlay to be bent dry, the inlay stock can be soaked and bent around a simple form until it is dry and it can then be glued in place.

With care and patience, you can cut the inlay stock on your power saw. If the material is too wide to fit in the router bit groove, it can be easily sanded down to the proper thickness with medium grade sandpaper.

When the inlay pattern is a vine with leaves, the stem of the vine is cut to the width of the router bit, usually 1/20 to 1/16 inch. The leaves are formed by drawing their outline and covering the entire area within the outline by moving the bit around within that area. The inlay stock is cut to the approximate shape of the leaves and can be accurately fitted to the area in a few minutes with sandpaper or fine pattern files.

Any good glue is satisfactory for gluing the inlay in place, however, the white glue in squeeze bottles is generally the most convenient to use. Contact cement is not suitable for use with inlay.

7

Special Problems in Window and Door Frames

7.1. Introduction

A rectangular frame with mitered corners has considerable application in furniture construction but the difficulty of constructing such a frame is much greater than one would expect. To construct such a frame, meeting accurately specified dimensions, with all corners right angles and with all four mitered joints making good contact over their entire lengths is not a simple feat of craftsmanship.

The reason that such an apparently simple structure is so difficult to fabricate is that the 45 degree angle must be cut accurately and the lengths of the members on opposite sides of the frame must be accurately the same. In addition, when a piece of lumber is cut at an angle, whether with a hand miter box or with a power saw, there is a component of force exerted parallel to the length of the piece of lumber which causes it to creep unless it is held very securely. This same force will tend to deflect the saw blade, whether it is a circular power saw or a hand saw in a miter box.

A miter joint is superior to a butt corner joint because the expansion and contraction of the joined surfaces will be the same during changes in relative humidity.

7.2. Cutting an Accurate Miter on a Power Saw

In order to cut an accurate miter on a power saw, four conditions must be satisfied. The miter gauge must be accurately set to cut an angle of 45 degrees, the workpiece must be held securely by the miter gauge, the saw must be accurately perpendicular to the saw table and the saw must be sufficiently rigid so that it will not be deflected appreciably while making the cut.

If the saw blade is subject to deflection while cutting the miter, the cut will not be accurate even though the workpiece is held securely and the miter gauge is properly set. It is seldom necessary to use a blade more than 8 inches in diameter for cutting miters and an 8 inch saw blade is less subject to deflection than a 10 or 12 inch saw blade of the same type. Since tapered blades are thinner than the other types, they should not be used for cutting miters. The blades with carbide tipped teeth are quite satisfactory and the special thick blades used for cutting tenons are especially good. The blade can be still further stiffened by adding stiffening washers. These are heavy steel washers, 4 inches in diameter, which can be placed on the two sides of the blade and are clamped firmly against it when the arbor nut is tightened. Figure 7.1 shows the arrangement, where *A* is the arbor, *B-B* are the stiffening washers, *C* is the arbor nut and *S* is the saw blade.

The miter gauges on most power saws have adjustable stops at the 90 degree and the two 45 degree positions. If you are purchasing a power saw, you should check the miter gauge to determine if it does have these stops. In some instances, there is a choice, with some price difference, between a simple miter gauge without stops and without a means of clamping the workpiece on the miter gauge and a more sophisticated one with stops and a means of

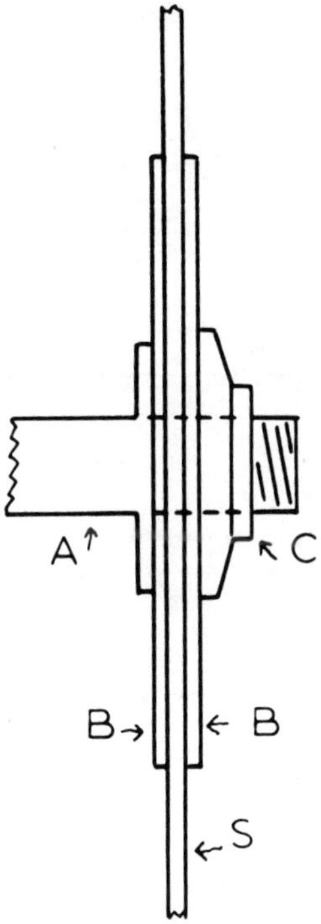

Fig. 7.1. A circular saw blade mounted on the arbor with stiffening washers.

clamping the workpiece. It is impossible to cut a sufficiently accurate miter with a simple miter gauge. If you have a saw equipped with only a simple miter gauge, you should purchase an adequate one before attempting to cut miters. Such a gauge will cost approximately $20.00 but it is a worthwhile investment and if you have one, remember that it is a precision device and should be handled with care.

It is, occasionally, necessary to adjust the stops on the miter gauge. Before starting to adjust these stops, the saw should be checked to be certain that it is perpendicular to the saw table. This can be done by raising the saw to near its maximum height and checking with a small square as indicated in Fig. 7.2, where *T* is the saw table, *S* is the saw

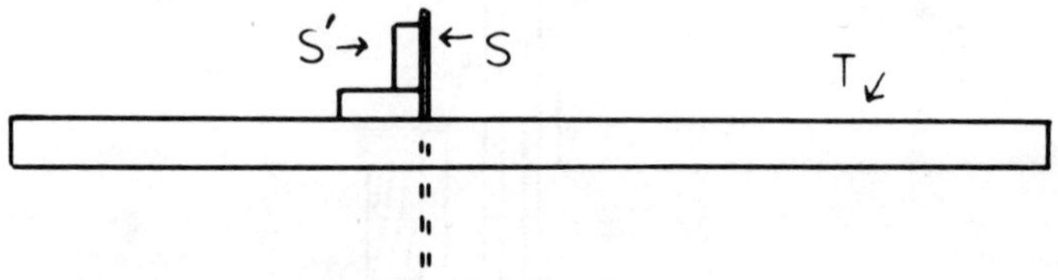

Fig. 7.2. Method of checking with a square to determine when the saw blade is perpendicular to the surface of the saw table.

blade and *S′* is the square. If you sight along the saw blade toward a light, you can determine when the edge of the square contacts the saw blade over its entire length. Of course, you should not use a tapered saw blade for this test or for cutting a miter.

Now, take a piece of lumber two or three inches wide with the edge to be held against the miter planed straight. Clamp the piece in the miter gauge, with the straight edge held firmly against the surface of the miter gauge after it has been turned to one of the 45 degree stops and saw the end off. Remove the piece and check with a combination square as indicated in Fig. 7.3. A slight deviation from a 45 degree angle can be detected by sighting across the surface *A* toward a light. If the blade of the square does not make contact along the entire length of the surface *A*, change the adjustment of the stop in the proper direction and make a second cut. Continue this until the blade of the square makes contact along the entire length of the surface *A*. When making the cuts, do not crowd the saw.

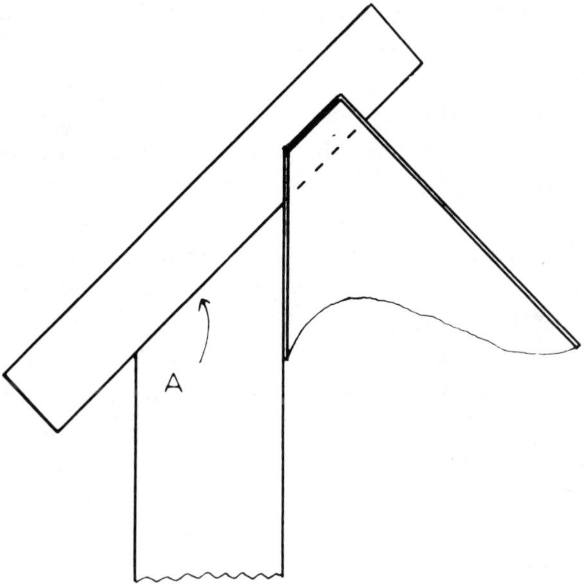

Fig. 7.3. Method of checking a miter with the combination square.

After the 45 degree stop is adjusted on one side, turn the miter gauge to the other 45 degree stop and adjust it in the same manner.

7.3. Cutting Miters with a Miter Box

A miter box consists of a frame for holding the workpiece with a guide for a back saw that can be set at various angles. In a miter box, the workpiece is held fixed in place while the saw is moved back and forth to make the cut. It is desirable to clamp the workpiece in place and the adjustment of the angle settings is done in a manner similar to that with a power saw.

Since the same kinds of forces are involved in cutting the miter on a miter box as are involved in making a corresponding cut with a power saw, the miter box must be constructed so that it has considerable strength and the saw must be very rigid. This is the reason for the high cost of a good miter box. A miter box capable of cutting accurate miters will cost approximately $75.00, but such a miter box is capable of cutting very accurate miters and many craftsmen prefer to use such a miter box rather than a power saw for precision work.

7.4. Cutting the Miters to Form an Accurate Rectangle

One of the requirements for producing an accurate set of miters to form the corners of a rectangle is that the lengths of the members on opposite sides of the rectangle must be equal. The requirement for equality of the lengths of these members is usually more stringent than the requirement for the absolute length of the members. It is much easier to cut a piece of lumber with square ends to a specific length than it is to cut the same piece to the same accuracy when the cut is made at an angle because of the manner in which the workpiece approaches the cutting edge of the saw.

To overcome this difficulty, it is desirable to cut the members for the opposite sides of the rectangle simultaneously. This can be done by stacking the two pieces with two or three drops of glue applied along their length between the surfaces and clamping them with the edges to be held against the face of the miter held firmly against a vertical surface. You can use the miter to hold the pieces until the glue dries and if white glue is used, this will require about 30 minutes. The miters on the ends of the two pieces can then be cut simultaneously and the two pieces will be the same length. They should be separated as soon as they are cut before the glue has had an opportunity to set to its maximum strength.

7.5. Gluing and Clamping the Frame

It is possible to purchase special corner clamps, four of which would be required to clamp the corners of a rectangular frame. Unfortunately, these clamps are relatively light and are not very satisfactory for large heavy frames.

It is possible to construct a clamping jig which can be used to clamp any size frame, using a single clamp to draw up the four corners. The four arms A_1, A_2, A_3 and A_4 in Fig. 7.4 are pivoted to the blocks B_1 and B_2 with bolts

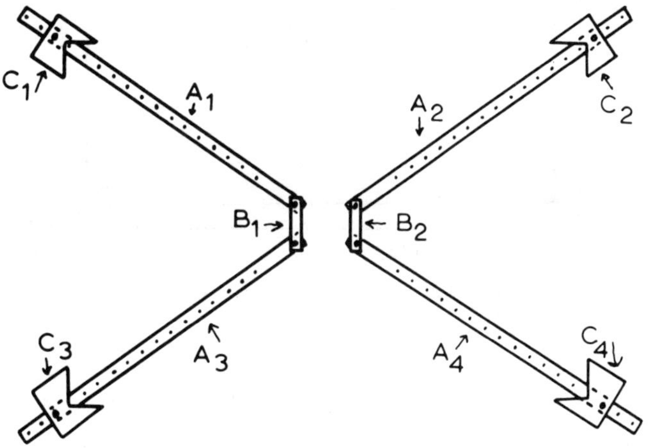

Fig. 7.4. A jig for clamping a rectangular frame with mitered joints at the corners.

which are loose enough so that the arms are free to pivot where they are joined to the blocks. The four blocks C_1,

C_2, C_3 and C_4 are attached to the arms A_1 - A_4 with screws in predrilled holes. The holes in the bars for accepting the screws should be drilled about one inch apart, starting the first hole in each bar the same distance from the hole which is used to attach the bars to the blocks *B*. It is a good idea to number the holes so that the blocks *C* can always be put at the same position on the arms *A* when clamping a frame. Before gluing, a dry run is made by mounting the frame in the jig as indicated in Fig. 7.5. As the clamp is tightened,

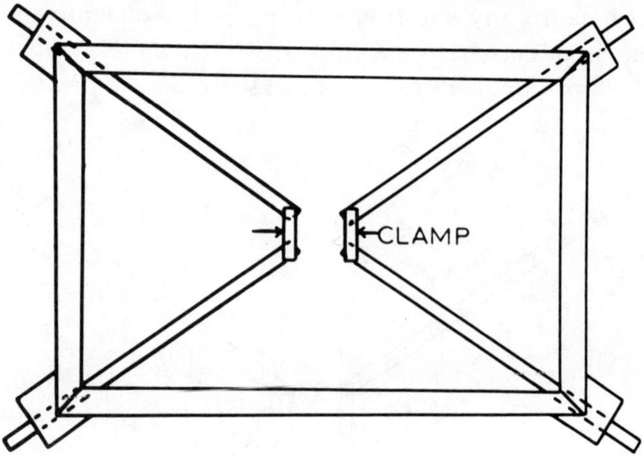

Fig. 7.5. The jig shown in Fig. 7.4 with a frame clamped in place.

It may be necessary to gently tap the corners with a mallet to overcome friction in the joints and cause the four corners of the frame to draw up to a perfect fit. After making the dry run with the frame, the clamp should be loosened, the frame carefully removed and the miters coated with glue and the frame carefully replaced in the jig after placing a piece of waxed paper on each corner of the jig under the miter joints to avoid gluing the frame to the jig with glue that squeezes out of the joints. The clamp is then tightened and the corners should draw up to a perfect fit.

7.6. Special Frames

The door to the face of a large clock is usually made with an arch at the top. There are three ways of constructing such a door as shown in Figs. 7.6, 7.7, and 7.8. The

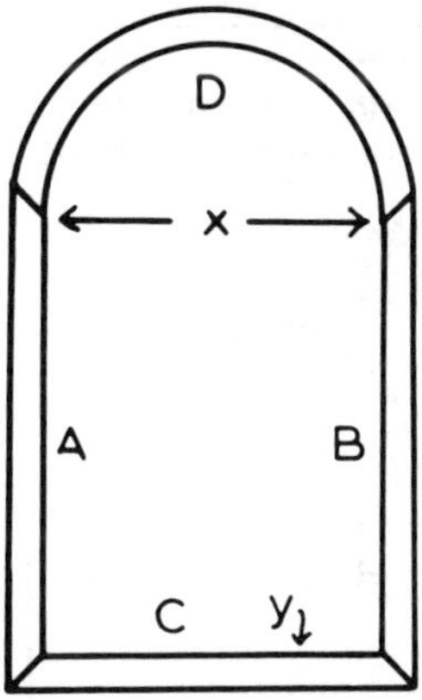

Fig. 7.6. A door with an arch at the top. The width of the arch is the same as the outside width of the frame.

particular design which is chosen will usually depend on the design of the rest of the case in which the door will be mounted. The design shown in Fig. 7.6 is the simplest to construct but there are not many instances where it can be used.

To construct such a frame, the sides *A* and *B* will have their top ends mitered to the arch D and their bottom ends mitered to the side C. You can cut the sides *A* and *B* with

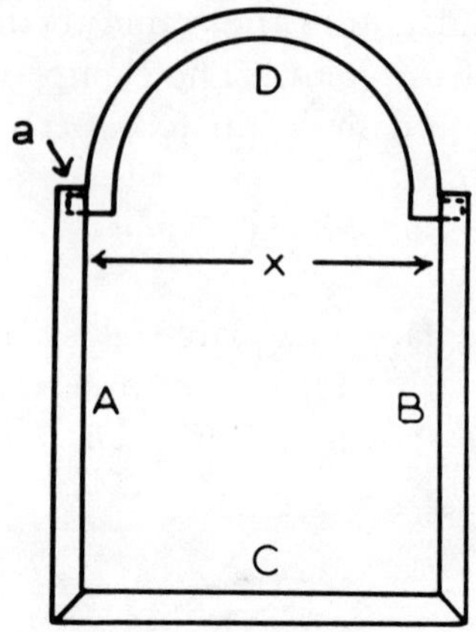

Fig. 7.7. A door with an arch at the top. The width of the arch is the same as the inside width of the frame.

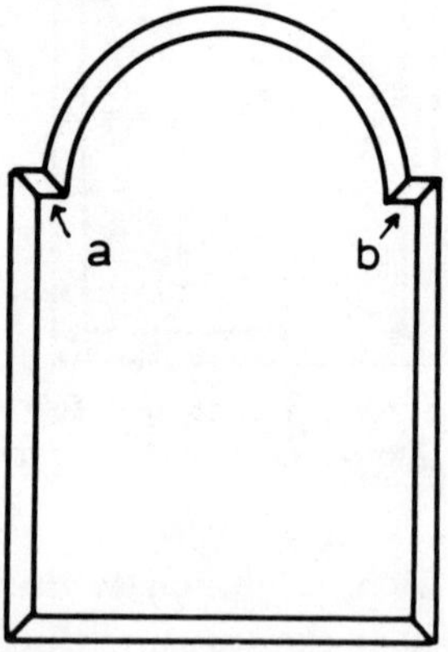

Fig. 7.8. A door with an arch at the top. The width of the arch is less than the inside width of the frame.

their ends mitered in the same manner as you would have cut these sides if they were to be the two sides of a rectangular frame.

You are going to need to cut the arch D from a solid piece of lumber with a band saw or a scroll saw. Figure 7.9 shows the layout of a piece of lumber from which the arch will be cut. The dotted lines show the outline of the arch and the line with arrows indicates the direction of the grain of the wood. Before cutting out the arch, you should cut the miters *a* and *b*. The length between these miters is the

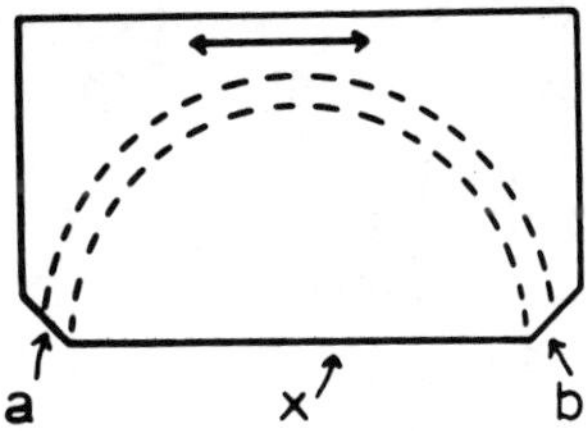

Fig. 7.9. Layout of the piece of lumber from which the arch for the door shown in Fig. 7.6 will be cut.

same as that of the side *C* so you can cut these miters simultaneously with the cutting of the side *C* by mounting the edge *x* of Fig. 7.9 and the edge *y* in Fig. 7.6 against the face of the miter gauge. You should, of course, attach the side *C* to the piece of lumber in Fig. 7.9 with a couple of drops of glue until these miters are cut. After the miters are cut the arch can be cut out following the dotted lines in Fig. 7.9.

Often such frames have a molding cut on the front of the inside edge and they also usually have a rabbet for mounting the glass front cut on the back of the inside edge. The inside curve of the arch should be cut first, the surface smoothed and the molding and the rabbet cut before the outside curve of the arch is cut. There are two reasons for doing it this way. First, on the sides of the arch, the grain of the wood is across the arch so it is not very strong and it can easily be broken by the forces of the molding and rabbet cutters. Second, it is much easier to hold the large piece of wood while cutting the molding and rabbet than it is to hold the narrow arch. After the molding and rabbet are cut, the cut can be made around the outside dotted line in Fig. 7.9 and the outside surface can be smoothed with a fine rasp and file.

The door frame shown in Fig. 7.7 is constructed in a different manner from that in Fig. 7.6. Only the bottom corners are mitered so side *C* and the miters on the bottom ends of sides *A* and *B* are cut and the top ends of sides *A* and *B* are squared.

The mortises at the tops of sides *A* and *B* are cut and sides *A, B* and *C* are laid out on a flat surface and the width *x* is carefully determined when the miters at the bottom corners are in perfect contact. This can be most easily done by making a simple jig like that shown in Fig. 7.10, where *A* is a piece of plywood somewhat larger than the door

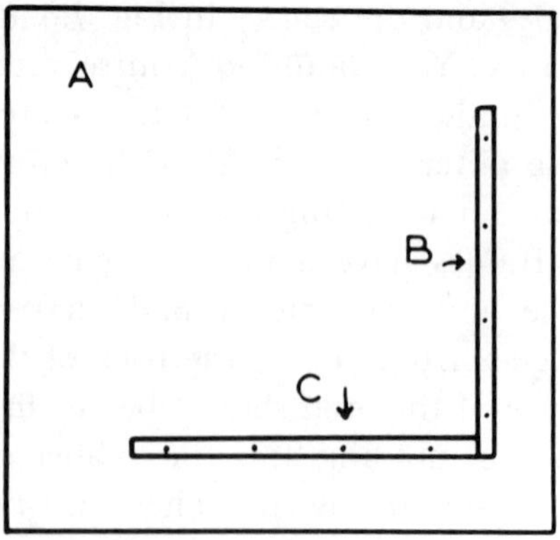

Fig. 7.10. A simple jig for use in laying out the arch for the door shown in Fig. 7.7.

frame and *B* and *C* are two straight strips of lumber nailed to the plywood so that they are accurately at right angles to each other.

The arch *D* is again cut from a solid piece of lumber. Figure 7.11 shows the layout for it. Since there are no

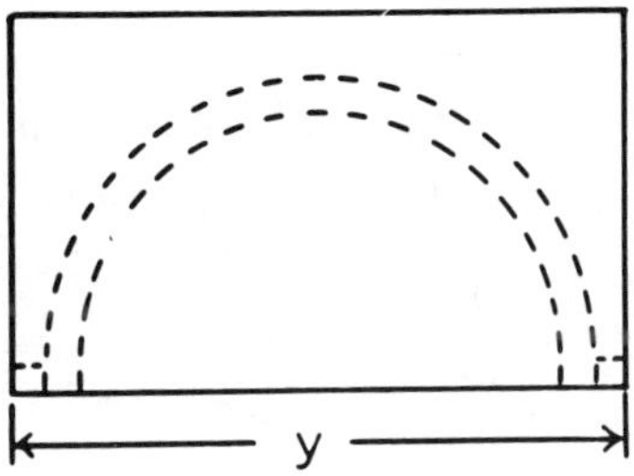

Fig. 7.11. Layout of the piece of lumber for cutting the arch for the door shown in Fig. 7.7.

miters on this piece, the length *y* will be equal to the length *x* in Fig. 7.7 plus the lengths of the two tenons. The inside curve of the arch should be cut first, smoothed and any moldings and rabbets cut. The outside of the arch is then cut leaving the width necessary for the tenons and, after smoothing the outside of the arch the tenons are formed. The cut along the line *a* in Fig. 7.12 should be made with a back saw.

There is an alternate method of forming the joints at the top of Fig. 7.7, which I prefer and which is easier to do than the more conventional arrangement. Instead of making mortise and tenon joints at the top, the piece in Fig. 7.11 can be accurately cut to the dimension *x* in Fig. 7.7 and the flat surfaces of *A* and *B* can be glued to the flat surfaces at the end of the arch when the frame is glued together. After the glue has set, two holes can be bored for

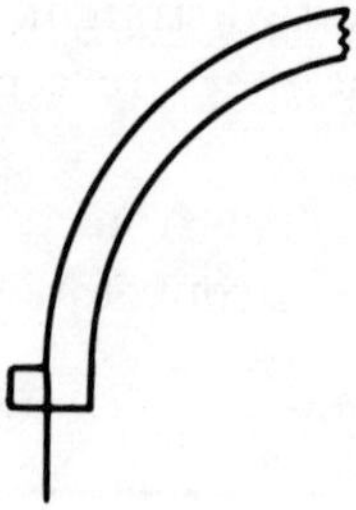

Fig. 7.12. Detail of the tenon on the arch for the door shown in Fig. 7.7.

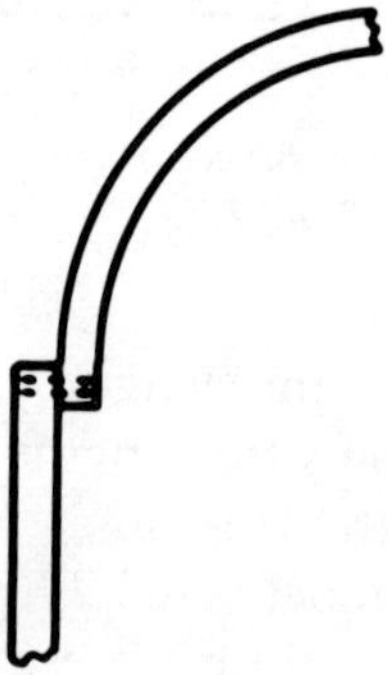

Fig. 7.13. Detail of an alternate method of attaching the arch for the door in Fig. 7.7.

1/4 inch dowel pins as indicated by the dotted lines in Fig. 7.13. The dowel pins can then be glued in place to provide the necessary reinforcing.

The door shown in Fig. 7.8 is the most difficult to construct but is more often used on large clocks with elaborate moldings. The door frame is much like the others except that at each of the top corners, the short pieces *a* and *b* in Fig. 7.8 join the sides of the frame to the arch at the top.

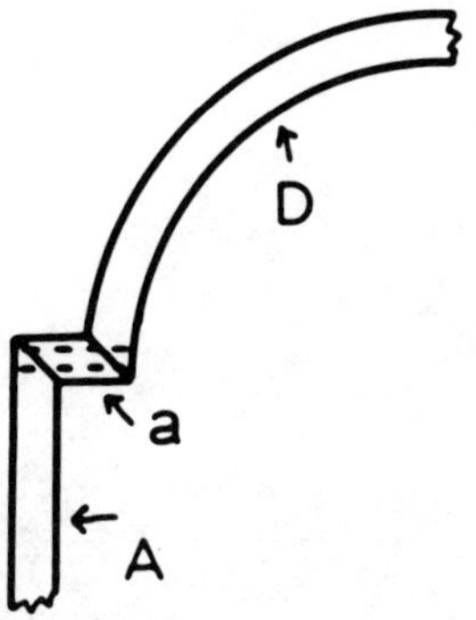

Fig. 7.14. Detail of dowel pin reinforcement for the top corner of the door shown in Fig. 7.8.

These pieces are difficult to cut because they are so short. The piece *a* in Fig. 7.14 should be cut from a longer piece which has had any molding and rabbet already cut on it. The miter which joins to the side *A* is cut first and the position of the cut for the miter which will join to the arch *D* is carefully marked. This second miter is then cut holding the longer length of the workpiece in the miter gauge. This second cut must be made with great care as it must be cut so that the absolute lengths of the pieces *a* and *b* are correct.

7.7. Assembling Special Clock Doors

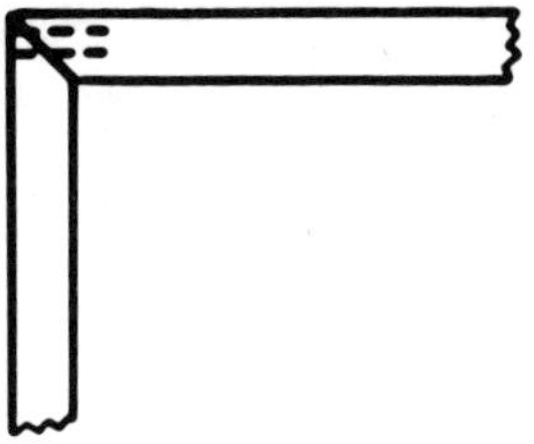

Fig. 7.15. Detail of dowel pin reinforcement of a mitered corner.

Fig. 7.16. The front of a Grandfather's clock face illustrating a door of the type shown in Fig. 7.8. All of the moldings on this clock except the cove at the bottom were cut with a molding cutter attachment on a drill press.

Since doors with arches at the top present a special problem of assembly, it is usually best to make a jig which will hold all of the pieces of the door in their proper position while they are being glued. The jig should be made so that the parts can be assembled flat on a piece of plywood with strips nailed in place to hold all of the components of the door in their proper orientation until the glue sets. In order to reinforce the corners of the door I prefer to bore two dowel pin holes of the appropriate size as indicated in Fig. 7.15 after the glue has set and glue in dowel pins to serve as reinforcement. The door shown in Fig. 7.14 can have the two mitered joints reinforced with a single pair of dowel pins by boring the holes through from the outside of the side *A* to the inside of the arch.

Figure 7.16 is a photograph of a clock front with a door like that in Fig. 7.8 which was constructed by the author. All of the moldings on this clock except the coves were cut with a molding cutter attachment on a drill press.

8

The Power Saw

8.1. Introduction

Of the various power tools, the power saw is the most useful. It is a precision tool but, in order to utilize its capabilities, it must be maintained in proper adjustment. The bench saw consists of a heavy cast iron table mounted on a frame which supports the bearings in which the arbor shaft rotates. The height of the saw blade relative to the top of the table is adjustable either by raising or lowering the arbor relative to the table or by raising or lowering the table relative to the arbor. There is also provision for either tilting the arbor or tilting the table to vary the angle of the blade surface relative to the top of the table.

Another kind of power saw is the radial arm saw in which the saw and the motor that drives it are supported on an arm above the table. The work is held stationary on the table while the saw is pushed through it except when long pieces are being ripped. In this chapter, I will confine the discussion primarily to the bench saw, as I am most familiar with its use. However, this discussion in combination with the manufacturer's manual for a radial arm saw should make it possible for an amateur to make the corresponding adjustments on the radial arm saw to do the various operations.

8.2. The Basic Adjustments of the Bench Saw

When the arbor or table is tilted to make cuts at an angle, a pointer is moved along an angle scale. When the saw blade is perpendicular to the saw table, the pointer should read at zero on the scale. In order to properly set the pointer, the saw should be raised to near its highest level and checked with a square as indicated in Fig. 7.2. The screw which holds the pointer can be loosened and the pointer can be turned to the zero division and the screw firmly tightened to hold the pointer in this position. For most cutting operations, the saw can be set to the zero position with sufficient accuracy by turning the angle setting crank until the pointer returns to zero. Where especially high accuracy cuts are to be made, the saw should be checked with a square as tilt angles too small to be detected on the angle scale can be detected by checking with a square.

Figure 8.1 shows the top of the saw table and *A* and *B* are the two grooves in which the miter slides. These grooves should be accurately parallel to the saw blade and this parallelism can be checked by measuring the distances *a* and *b*. Unless the saw has been subjected to severe usage, the original adjustment made at the factory will still be correct. However, if the distances *a* and *b* are not the same, the bolts holding the table to the frame should be loosened and the table should be tapped with a mallet at either corner *C* or *D* until the distances *a* and *b* are equal. The bolts holding the table to the frame should then be firmly tightened.

In Fig. 8.1, *F* is the fence and *E* is the bar along which the tee of the fence travels as the distance between the saw and the fence is varied. There is a means of adjustment of the angle between the fence and the tee that will vary with

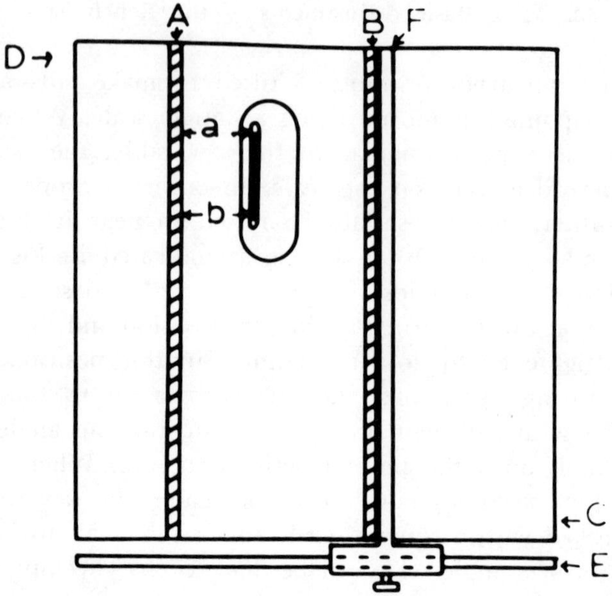

Fig. 8.1. Saw table illustrating adjustments of the table orientation and adjustment of the fence.

the make and model of the saw. If the edge of the fence is not parallel with the groove *B* when the fence is clamped in the position indicated in Fig. 8.1, the locking screws should be loosened so that the fence can be adjusted to parallelism with the groove *B*. The screws should then be securely tightened. This adjustment insures that the fence will be parallel to the saw blade.

In the preceding chapter, the adjustment of the miter stops for the 45 degree angle cuts was described. The adjustment for the 90 degree position is done in the same manner except that the stop is adjusted until a piece of lumber, when sawed with the miter set at the 90 degree position, will check square when tested with a square.

Most saws have a scale to indicate the depth of cut of the saw blade. It is usually not practical to consider setting the index of this scale to zero when the saw blade is just flush with the top of the saw table unless you work entirely with one blade because two blades of the same specified diameter will often differ somewhat in actual diameter.

You should determine by test, if it is not specified, how much difference in depth of cut corresponds to one division on the scale. You can accurately measure the depth of cut for any particular setting by sawing across a piece of scrap lumber. You can then calculate the amount you must change the depth scale reading to obtain any desired depth of cut.

8.3. Use of the Saw to Straighten Twisted or Warped Pieces of Lumber

Often, one has a twisted or warped piece of lumber which must be straightened before it can be used. This can be done by making a pair of straight runners slightly thicker than the board to be straightened and slightly longer than the board as indicated in Fig. 8.2, where *A* is the board

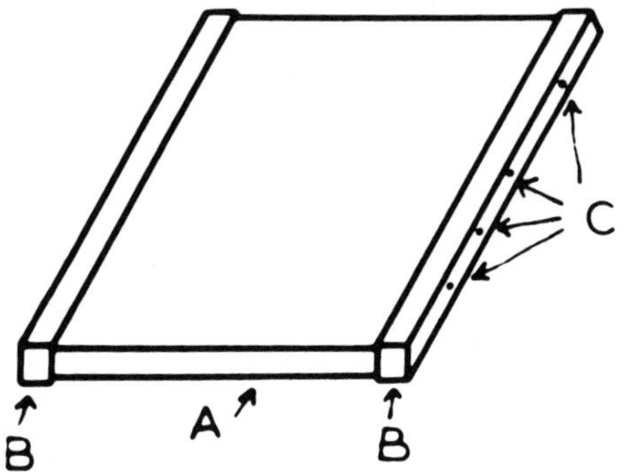

Fig. 8.2. Jig for straightening a warped or twisted board on a saw.

and *B - B* are the runners. The runners are placed on the saw table and the board is placed between them. The runners are attached to the edges of the board by means of the nails *C*. The high areas on both sides of the board are cut down to the level of the lowest areas by using the planer blades on the molding head and making successive cuts by sliding the runners on the surface of the table using the fence as a guide. The fence is first set so that a shallow cut is made along one edge of the board, and it is then moved a distance equal to the width of the cutters and a second cut is made. This process is repeated until the entire surface of the board is contacted by the cutter. The cutter is then lowered, the unit is turned over and the process is repeated on the other side. The runners *B* in Fig. 8.2 should be made wider than the grooves for the miter on the saw table so that they can pass over the grooves without dropping into them.

This same arrangement can be used as a means of planing a board down to a reduced thickness. Great care must be exercised to be certain that the nails *C* in Fig. 8.2 are located so that they will not be contacted by the planer blades.

The same procedure can be followed with a radial arm saw; the only difference is that the cuts with the radial arm saw will be made on the top of the board instead of on the bottom.

8.4. Resawing

Resawing is the process of cutting thin boards from thicker ones. Figure 8.3 shows the arrangement for resawing with a bench saw, where *T* is the saw table, *F* is the fence and *A* is the piece of lumber being resawed. It is important to check the side of the fence with a square to be certain that its face is perpendicular to the table so that the piece

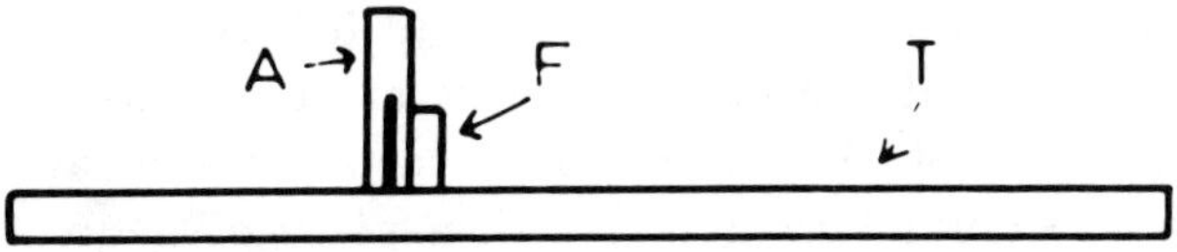

Fig. 8.3. Arrangement for resawing.

of lumber will not be tapered. With a 10 inch bench saw, it is possible to resaw lumber up to about 2 3/4 inches wide with a single cut. A 5 1/2 inch piece of lumber can be cut by resawing to the maximum depth of the saw from one edge and then a second cut is made from the other edge. Of course, the same side of the piece of lumber must be held against the fence for both cuts.

8.5. Cutting Tenons

A method commonly used in cutting tenons is shown in Fig. 8.4, where *T* is the saw table, *M* is the miter, *A* is the piece on which the tenon is being cut and *B* is the molding

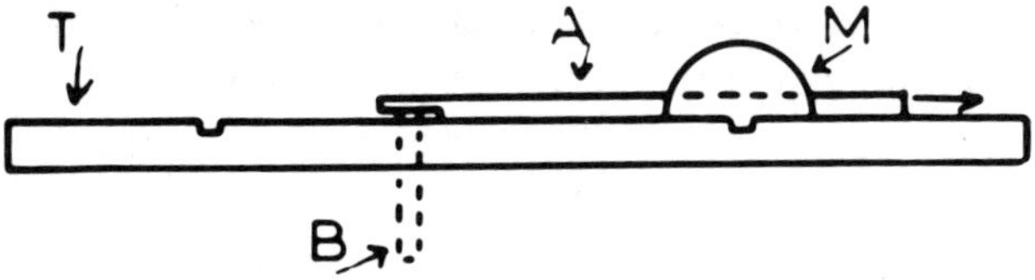

Fig. 8.4. A method of cutting a tenon.

head with planar type blades. Successive cuts are made, moving the piece *A* in the direction of the arrow between successive cuts. It is possible to cut the tenon with a saw blade such as a carbide tipped blade. However, the piece *A* can then be moved only about 1/8 inch between successive cuts. Since the depth of cut is quite critical in forming the tenon, the height of the molding cutter or the saw above the table should be checked with a piece of scrap lumber before starting to cut the tenon.

An alternate method of cutting a tenon is shown in Fig. 8.5, where *T* is the saw table, *A* is the piece on which the

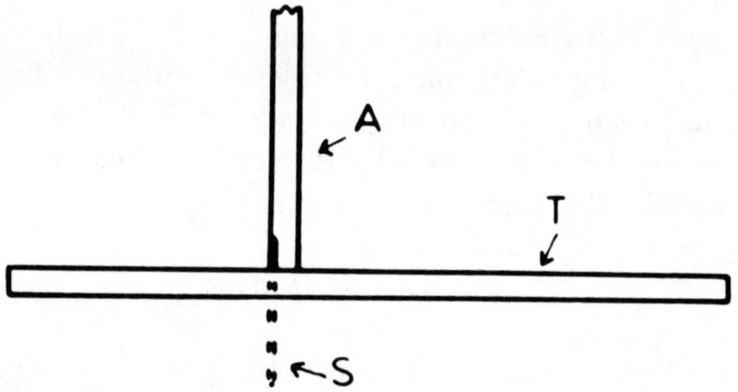

Fig. 8.5. An alternate method of cutting a tenon.

tenon is being cut and *S* is the saw. In this method, the piece is held vertically and the saw is raised above the table by an amount equal to the length of the tenon. To use this method, a means of holding and accurately guiding the piece *A* is essential. It is possible to purchase a tenon jig which has a bar on the bottom which slides in one of the miter grooves on the saw table. Figure 8.6 shows the mechanical arrangement of the jig. The plate *C* slides on the saw table and it is guided by means of the bar *B* which slides in the miter slot. The part *D* can slide in the direction of the arrows on the plate *C*. Guides are provided to insure that the motion is perpendicular to the bar *B* and a lock nut is provided so that it can be locked in the desired

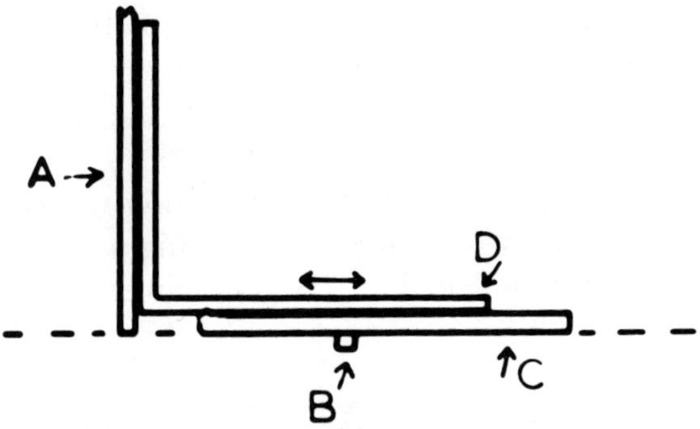

Fig. 8.6. A tenon jig for holding a board for cutting a tenon as illustrated in Fig. 8.5.

position. A vertical guide and clamps are provided for the vertical portion of part *D* so that the piece *A*, on which the tenon is to be cut, can be clamped vertically to the face of the part *D*. This is a very convenient means of cutting tenons.

It is possible to construct a simple tenon jig which uses the saw fence as a guide. Figure 8.7 shows such a jig, where

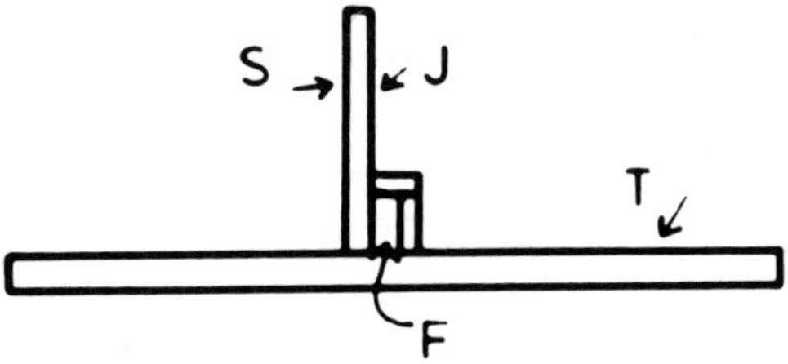

Fig. 8.7. A home made tenon jig.

T is the saw table, *F* is the fence and *J* is the jig which is constructed so that it straddles the fence and can slide along the fence. The piece on which the tenon is to be cut can be clamped to the surface *S* with a *C* clamp. It is helpful to attach a vertical strip to the surface *S* with screws to help in properly aligning the piece on which the tenon is to be cut.

A tenon jig is very convenient for cutting straight tenons, but it is particularly convenient for cutting a dovetail tenon such as that indicated in Fig. 8.8. The dovetails are usually

Fig. 8.8. A dovetail tenon.

cut at an angle of 15 degrees, so the saw can be tilted to an angle of 15 degrees and the dovetail tenon is cut following the same procedure as for a straight tenon. A horizontal cut should be made at the base of the tenon before the piece is mounted in the tenon jig.

8.6. Cutting Tapers

It is possible to purchase a special jig for cutting tapers on a power saw. However, the problem most often encountered by the amateur is that of cutting the taper on a table leg. Usually the taper on a table leg is specified in terms of the dimensions at the top and bottom of the taper. A simple jig can be constructed like that shown in Fig. 8.9, where *A* is a straight piece of lumber two or three inches wide and 1/2 or 3/4 inch thick. The distance between the blocks *B* and *C* is equal to the length of the leg.

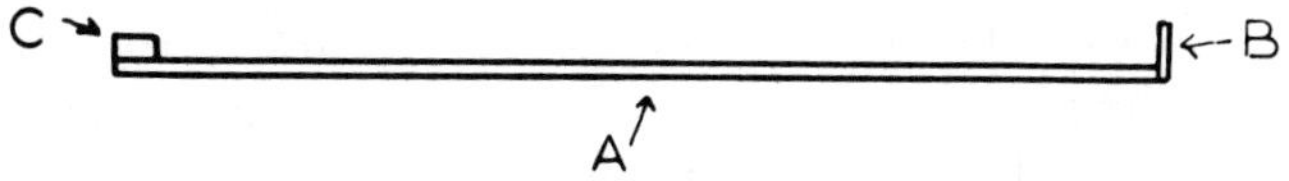

Fig. 8.9. A home made jig for cutting a taper on a table leg.

To cut a taper, arrange the setup as indicated in Fig. 8.10, where *T* is the saw table, *F* is the fence, *A* is the strip *A* in Fig. 8.9 and *L* is the table leg. In some instances, a leg is tapered all the way from the bottom to the top while in others, the taper extends to some point *a* below the top. If *w* is the width to be cut away at the bottom, the leg should

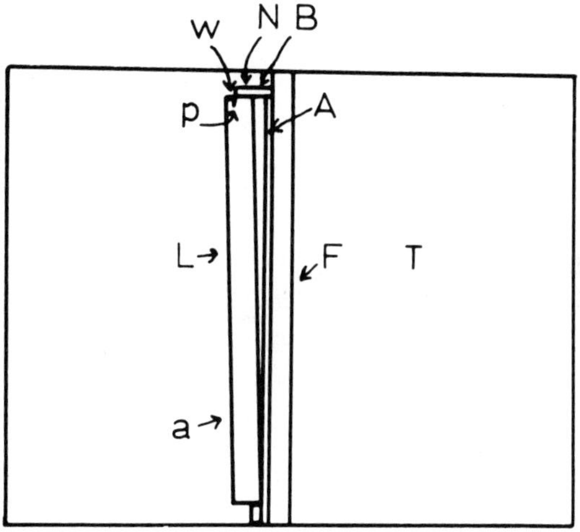

Fig. 8.10. Arrangement for using the jig shown in Fig. 8.9 on the table saw.

be separated from the jig at the bottom until the distance from the fence to *p* is the same as the distance from the fence to *a*. The block *B* can be attached to the bottom of the leg with a nail *N* to hold it in that orientation. The fence is then adjusted until, when the jig and leg are advanced to the saw, it will cut away the width *w* at the bottom. As the unit is pushed through the saw, it will come out of the leg at the point *a*. If the leg is to be tapered on only two adjacent sides, the nail *N* can be removed, the leg is rotated 90 degrees and the nail can be driven in again with the spacing between the leg and the fence the same as it was for the first cut.

If the taper is to be cut on all four sides, the width *w* in Fig. 8.10 will be only half as great for each cut as it was when the taper was cut on only two sides.

Glossary

ARBOR: A metal shaft or axis on which a revolving cutting tool, such as a saw, is mounted.

BACK SAW: A fine toothed saw stiffened by a metal rib along its back edge.

BURNISHING TOOL: A round hardened steel tool used for forming the edge of a scraper.

CABRIOLE LEG: A form of furniture leg frequently used in Queen Anne and Chippendale furniture that curves outward from the structure which it supports and then descends in a tapering reverse curve terminating in an ornamental foot.

COMBINATION SQUARE: A measuring tool consisting of a steel rule that slides through an adjustable protractor head.

COVE: A molding with a concave cross section.

DRAW KNIFE: A woodworker's tool having a blade with a handle at each end.

FENCE: An attachment to a saw or other woodworking machine that controls the location of a cut.

GOUGE: A tool with a concavo-convex cross section used for scooping or cutting holes channels or grooves.

HEADSTOCK: Bearing or pedestal holding the revolving shaft of a lathe.

JIG: A device used to maintain, mechanically, the correct positional relationship between a piece of work and a tool or, between parts of work during assembly.

MARKING GAUGE: A carpenter's tool for scribing a line parallel to the edge of a piece of work.

MILL FILE: A metal cutting file.

MITER GAUGE: A tool with graduations used to set a saw or a piece to be sawed to any desired angle.

MITER JOINT: A joint made by fastening together parts with the ends cut at an angle.

MORTISE: A hole groove or slot into which another part can be fitted.

PATTERN FILES: Small variously shaped fine files used for shaping small parts.

SAW KERF: A slot cut into the end of a piece with a saw.

SCROLL SAW: A thin hand saw held in a rectangular frame for cutting curves.

SPINDLE: A slender round rod often used in forming the back of a chair, also, the vertical rotating shaft and its stationary housing in a drill press.

SPLAT: A single flat thin member in a chair back.

TAILSTOCK: The stationary workholder on the opposite end of a lathe from the headstock.

TENON: A projection on a piece of wood or other material shaped to fit a mortise.

VEE BLOCK: A block with a top surface shaped like the letter V often used for holding round pieces on the table of a drill press.

Index